THE INSURED PORTFOLIO

THE INSURED PORTFOLIO

Your Gateway to Stress-Free Global Investments

ERIKA NOLAN
MARC-ANDRÉ SOLA
SHANNON CROUCH

John Wiley & Sons, Inc.

Published by John Wiley & Sons, Inc., Hoboken, New Jersey.

Published simultaneously in Canada.

For general information on our other products and services or for technical support, please contact our Customer Care Department within the United States at (800) 762-2974, outside the United States at (317) 572-3993 or fax (317) 572-4002.

Wiley also publishes its books in a variety of electronic formats. Some content that appears in print may not be available in electronic books. For more information about Wiley products, visit our web site at www.wiley.com.

Library of Congress Cataloging-in-Publication Data:

Nolan, Erika.
    The insured portfolio: your gateway to stress free global investments/Erika Nolan, Shannon Crouch, Marc-Andre Sola.
       p. cm.
    Includes bibliographical references and index.
    ISBN 978-0-470-57514-7 (cloth); 978-0-470-87568-1 (ebk);
    978-0-470-87567-4 (ebk)
  1. Portfolio management.   2. Global Financial Crisis, 2008–2009.   I. Crouch, Shannon.   II. Sola, Marc-Andre.   III. Title.
    HG4529.5.C76 2010
    332.6—dc22   2010009568

Printed in the United States of America

10 9 8 7 6 5 4 3 2 1

DISCLAIMER

While the authors have used their best efforts in preparing this book, they make no representations or warranties with respect to the accuracy or completeness of the contents of this book and specifically disclaim any implied warranties of merchantability or fitness for a particular purpose. No warranty may be created or extended by sales representatives or written sales materials. The advice and strategies contained herein may not be suitable for your situation. You should consult with a professional where appropriate. Neither the publisher nor authors shall be liable for any loss of profit or any other commercial damages, including but not limited to special, incidental, consequential, or other damages.

CONTENTS

ACKNOWLEDGMENTS

We would like to express our sincere thanks to many people who either helped to create this book or supported us during the process.

Shannon Crouch: Thanks to all The Sovereign Society members I have met over the years for sharing their successes, failures, and perspectives on wealth. You have helped refine the solutions offered within these pages. Thanks to The Sovereign Society team for supporting my time away from the office to write this book. And to my soon-to-be husband, Spike, as well as my parents, thank you for your unending support of me and the projects that mean so much to me.

Erika Nolan: Thank you to Bob Kephart and Robert Bauman, whose vision gave birth to The Sovereign Society so many years ago. Their mentorship gave me the passion, the opportunity, and the experience to write this book with my colleagues. Thanks to The Sovereign Society team for allowing me to dedicate time to this book. I must also thank Patrick, Bianca, and my mother for their undying support of this project and of me.

Marc-André Sola: I thank my parents for allowing me to study and get a good education. I would also like to thank Jürg Lattmann for being my first mentor and for getting me into the industry; Maria Amstad for being my long-time business partner and helping me build the business; and Dr. Josef Haid, my friend and loyal business partner, for allowing me to be away from work while I wrote my share of the book.

Collectively, we would like to thank John Wiley & Sons for their patience and their belief that offshore solutions do work for the average investor. Without them, this information would not be so easily available.

A NEW GENERATION OF SAVERS AND INVESTORS HAVE BROUGHT CERTAINTY TO THEIR FINANCIAL FUTURE—AND SO CAN YOU!

We don't have any illusions.

We know you probably wouldn't have picked up this book if it were not for the financial crisis of the past few years coupled with the unprecedented government response that followed. And, honestly, had those events not taken place, we probably wouldn't have written it. For virtually every one of us wants nothing more than endless sunshine and a continuously rising Dow Jones average.

Some of us even have come to expect it.

Unfortunately, this mentality has allowed retirement accounts, family savings, and investor nest eggs to become easy fatalities. The profits of yesteryear are starting to return, but we investors are now much more jaded—and rightfully so.

Most of us grew up during a period the French call *Les Trente Glorieuses* (The Glorious Thirty, 1945–1975). The term was coined by a French demographer who watched firsthand as the country—decimated by two world wars—rose to have the highest standard of living worldwide in the early 1970s. Likewise, the United States and the United Kingdom enjoyed decades of relatively uninterrupted prosperity in that same period. Those decades were brimming with prosperity for citizens of most Western economies.

Most of us weren't around for the Great Depression, so we couldn't comprehend how far or just how fast the economy could crumble. And only a few of us appreciate how the Second World War decimated industrial competition from countries like Germany and Japan and how that positioned the United States to lead the world economy during the 1950s and 1960s.

So where does it leave us? It leaves us with a generation of people who are less financially spry than their forefathers of previous generations. Much like the age of Pax Romana hid the deeper truth of the Roman Empire's slow decay and ultimate collapse, so, too, have the *Les Trente Glorieuses* masked a more complicated truth for Western societies.

FIGHT OR FLIGHT—THE COURAGE TO SEE BEYOND

But let us be clear; this book is not about fear mongering.

It's not about the one-in-a-million scenarios passed off as the inevitable future or one isolated event that will lead to our widespread demise. Yet, we don't believe fear is necessarily a bad thing; often, your sense of fear keeps you safe. But heaven knows there's already too much fear being pushed upon us in the news, on the radio, and on virtually every TV show. While there *is* a certain amount of honesty to it, fear isn't the problem.

Uncertainty is the problem.

If you were certain about what was going to happen in the future, you'd have absolutely nothing to fear. Horrible accidents, disasters, stock market crashes—knowing about these things ahead of time would allow you to prepare accordingly. While absolute certainty is impossible, if you at least had an idea about the *likelihood* of something threatening you or your wealth, you'd be much better off to protect yourself against it. You'd take steps to give yourself some insurance just in case the worst scenario came to pass.

And that's what this book is about.

It's about preparing yourself for the immense financial uncertainties you face as a saver or an investor in the twenty-first century. We reveal the major financial threats and reasons why you must act to insure your wealth, plus give you clear actions to take.

Think of this book as a tool to help you analyze your personal financial situation, asking all the relevant questions and answering them comprehensively.

In the first chapter, we'll focus on each of the culprits responsible for the uncertainty in your financial future. We'll talk about everything from the new generation of empowered crooks to the chefs who cooked the golden goose—the government, of course.

But we're not just telling you how we have gotten to this point; we're offering solutions. The second chapter of this book focuses on what *you* will need to respond to these threats. The world has grown much entwined since the *Les Trente Glorieuses*, and this creates significant threats and also amazing opportunities to those of us who explore them. It means that, for many of us, the traditional portfolio of American stocks and bonds will simply not cut it anymore. It will not allow us to sleep well at night knowing our retirement will be a reality or that we will be able to sustain a legacy (no matter how great or small) for our families. But there are solutions that will give you peace of mind regardless of what uncertainties abound.

From Chapter 4 onward, we'll zero in on the best-fit solutions for savers and investors looking to get ahead in the twenty-first century. We'll cover every detail of every opportunity, with case studies to match. You will be able to see how these solutions can work for someone in your situation.

It is our sincere hope that the insight contained on these pages will help quiet the doubts you may have developed about your financial future, and that it gives you at least one clear path to relative certainty and greater peace of mind. There's a chance it might drastically improve your fortunes.

CHAPTER 1

WELCOME TO THE TWENTY-FIRST CENTURY

The Lessons of the First Decade and the Historical Precedent for Today's "Unprecedented" Crisis

It was a crazy year.

In 12 short months, the world's ruling empire saw a widespread mortgage crisis, shocking the financial system and sending interbank lending rates through the roof. Complex financial instruments collapsed like a house of cards, and overleveraged businesses suffered. If their short-term loans came due and they couldn't refinance, that was it. Locks appeared on the doors, and the windows were papered.

Through it all, however, a handful of new countries shone. These nations were growing thanks to lower wages, cheaper commodities, and looser regulations. Financial supremacy started to shift as the world looked for a new center of power. Across the ocean they found one.

We're not talking about 2008, by the way.

We're talking about 1873, at the beginning of what some historians call the *real* Great Depression. And that promising new center of power was the United States.

HISTORY MAY NOT REPEAT . . .

. . . But it certainly rhymes.

And in this case, it's rhymed pretty closely so far. The similarities are staggering, even though the participants may have changed. And while the Great Depression brought about a revolution in big government and interventions, the Crash of 1873 embodied the end of an era—something we're almost certainly witnessing now. Let us explain.

In the decade leading up to 1873, Europe saw the rise of the Austro-Hungarian Empire and the unification of the German states. Combined with France, it was believed that these countries would help Europe retain its status as financial center of the universe.

In reality, the continent's financial system was already overstretched.

Thanks to the amiable political atmosphere, new lending institutions were sprouting like weeds. Much like the decades leading up to 2008, these lenders relaxed terms and issued obscene amounts of mortgages, leading to a building boom and soaring prices in residential and municipal real estate. The capital cities of Berlin, Paris, and Vienna were at the center of the boom.

Fast forward to the United States, 2008. For many years prior, mortgages were readily handed out, and as home prices began to skyrocket, speculators began to use other houses—some even yet unbuilt—as collateral for more loans in the years leading up to the correction.

In both 1873 and 2008, the panic was touched off by a rash of bank insolvencies.

By May 1873, the Viennese stock market had crashed. British investors started pulling back their funds, for fear that any or all of these continental banks might themselves soon be insolvent. Entire markets for complex, principal-guaranteed derivatives collapsed overnight. Interbank lending rates soared to impossibly high levels, and the world's financial markets became a ticking time bomb.

American railroad companies, much like the overleveraged private equity firms of today, were the first to feel the pinch. Their dependence on the short-term credit markets, now frozen by the crisis in

Europe, meant that it was only a matter of time before the cash would run out for many firms. In September of that year, the bankruptcy of Wall Street mainstay Jay Cooke over a failed railroad bond auction was all it took to send America's stock market crashing.

WHY THE EVENTS OF 1873 REALLY MATTER

You see, the developments and events of 1873—and their striking similarity to 2008—are merely quirky anecdotes compared to what followed.

It had vast implications. The panic would lay the groundwork for America's global dominance in the twentieth century.

At the time, the cheap grain and kerosene exports coming from the United States were equivalent to the cheap goods from China we depend on today. Thanks to a number of factors, including weak government regulation, low taxes, and some of the lowest wages in the global economy, American producers could undercut domestic alternatives in most countries. In the case of Britain, for example, almost the entire country was dependent on cheap grain exports from the United States.

As the United States grew into its new role as global supplier of basic consumer goods, Americans began building a mountain of savings. This was in stark contrast to the mountain of debt being built in Europe, where the "financial center of the universe" allegedly resided. The difference became more apparent as the years rolled on, though most people only minded the short term, not understanding the commonsense implications of what was playing out in the long term.

When the crash finally came in 1873, it was too late for Europe to do much, if anything, to stop it. In the long term, the continent's status as financial capital of the world slowly shifted overseas, to where American savings could restore global growth without the aid of fickle credit, and to where an honest, hard-working economy was creating real wealth that would lead the world into a new century.

If history rings true, the same global shift is under way now.

AMERICA'S AGE AS A SUPERPOWER

If history is our guide, then 1873 and 2008 may well be the bookends of America's story as a global superpower: financially, politically, and militarily. Each historic crisis signaled a much deeper, centuries-long shift in global dominance from one nation to another.

But you will recall that power wanes slowly. The Austro-Hungarian Empire didn't descend into ruin immediately after the crash. Europe's fortunes would wane slowly in the wake of 1873, but the continent was never reduced to a global backwater.

In comparison, 2008 saw the U.S. federal government issuing unprecedented fiscal and monetary stimulus that has stemmed the short-term consequences of the recent crash, yet at the risk of making some of its long-term consequences far worse. Indeed, the U.S. government has been so successful—and gone to such great expense at maintaining appearances—that it may for years continue to appear that nothing has changed. But the reality is that the power shift will already be well under way.

THE GENERATIONAL WEALTH PHENOMENON

There is Chinese proverb that extols the reality of building real wealth.

It says, *"Wealth does not pass three generations."* The first generation of wealth will be lucky and perseverant, hardworking and diligent in saving for their family. The second generation will not face the same challenges. While it enjoys the fruits of the first generation's hard work, it will fail to appreciate the work that goes into building wealth. And by the third generation, the wealth will be squandered. This is a phenomenon that is all too common and one that we will focus on throughout the book.

Look not only to the wealthy American families, but to America's auto industry or even the *New York Times*, and you will see this effect playing out on an epic scale. But for the purposes of this book, let's take a quick look at America as a whole, in the three generations between 1873 and 2008. Skewing the usual topics of politics, industry, and the economy from this perspective will help to focus your own long-term thinking, helping you appreciate the appropriate scale and depth of an investment horizon of 30 years or more.

THE FIRST GENERATION: PRIOR TO THE 1920s— LIVING THE AMERICAN DREAM

In the time between 1873 and FDR's New Deal in 1933, it might appear that Americans were still chasing the American dream. But, in reality, they were living it.

The American dream isn't about the suburbs, cookouts, and family sedans of the 1950s. It isn't about home ownership. These things are the trappings of the American dream, the fruits of it. The real American dream is free enterprise.

You see, this generation of Americans cleverly understood the importance of peace of mind. When you don't have to worry about protecting the spoils of your labor from some other party, you can work that much harder. Free of distraction and impediments, you can truly have full dedication to your pursuits—the unvarnished incentive to be the best you possibly can be. And if your labors are fruitful, you can use the resulting wealth and your own keen insight to contribute to the growth of the economy at large. You can innovate, create jobs, and effect vast changes to the landscape that will ensure your place in history.

That's the kind of freedom at the heart of the real American dream. And that freedom was alive and well in the years after 1873. Americans saw the invention of the light bulb, the assembly line, the first manned flight, and the first stages of a national energy and communications infrastructure. Its country was a bustling new superpower, eagerly rushing into the transformative twentieth century.

The turn of the century saw the birth of many recognizable companies that still dominate the marketplace today: Eastman Kodak, Firestone Tire and Rubber Company, Hershey's, U.S. Steel, Monsanto Chemical Company, Ford Motor Company, JCPenney Corporation, and Pepsi.

At the time, the government was receptive to growth and didn't present any roadblocks. Before the New Deal, government spending scarcely comprised more than 10 to 15 percent of the economy and was vastly overshadowed by the dominance of the private sector.

Likewise, prior to 1915, tax rates were lower at this time than any other point in the twentieth century, with a top marginal tax rate of 7 percent for those with incomes in excess of $500,000. The exception, of course, was during World War I, when taxes were raised to more than 70 percent.

But things were not perfect.

Workers enjoyed very few protections or entitlements, and in especially competitive labor markets, people were often abused or exploited. There were few regulatory bodies monitoring or ensuring the safety of manufactured goods, financial products, or loan activity. By the booming 1920s, this generation was hitting its peak on the heels of a massive real estate and infrastructure explosion that helped bring about the indebtedness pivotal to the Great Depression. Nonetheless, this is the generation where real wealth was made.

THE SECOND GENERATION: 1920s–1970s—KILLING THE GOLDEN GOOSE

Thanks to the prosperity created by the first generation, the second generation spent years living comfortably or, at the very least, watched their neighbors do so. And then, much like now, they counter-intuitively demanded a government that could help them protect and preserve that comfort level, even when faced with common economic cycles and disruptions. They became so accustomed to the *trappings* of the American dream that, to them, the dream was almost meaningless without them.

In short, they had it good—and they had the clout to demand even better, even if it was unsustainable.

Out of Crisis: A New Breed of Leader

It was around this same time that, in a number of ways, the job of the American politician changed significantly.

The role of a politician became remarkably similar to any other top executive of the twentieth century. The executive risked losing his job if he didn't keep the shareholders happy, and the politicians had to please voters or risk losing them. They both faced extreme pressure to generate a constant stream of consistent short-term results. And the stiffer the competition, the more outstanding and effective those results had to be.

Thus, as Americans faced catastrophe, they continuously urged the government to step in and make life a little easier for themselves and their fellow man. During the hard times, citizens insisted on increased government spending to stimulate the economy—an idea ushered onto the political stage by John Maynard Keynes, and one that would have a lasting impact on the way politicians deal with the economy even today.

Consequentially, some of America's most successful executives *and* politicians make similar kinds of decisions. In general, they tended to favor fast results at the expense of unknown implications—a kind of "buy now, pay later" mentality. To show you what we mean, let's start with one of the first examples of this new kind of political mentality: the New Deal.

Short-Term Solutions that Never Went Away

We are not going to discount the severity of the Great Depression or the necessity for the government to find short-term solutions to do something about it. In fact, we won't even argue the need for those types of programs. Faced with unemployment rates near 30 percent, thousands of banks failing, and millions of Americans who had lost everything, the actions the government took *were* necessary to provide relief to an affected generation. What wasn't necessary, however, was the continuation of those programs toward their inevitable demise.

For example, in 1938, FDR's administration had a simple goal. They needed a short-term solution to get people back on their feet. As borrowers defaulted on mortgages en masse and banks found themselves strapped for cash, President Franklin D. Roosevelt and Congress created Fannie Mae in order to buy mortgages from lenders. Fannie would give lenders, such as banks, cash for loans conforming to Fannie Mae guidelines, thus keeping mortgage rates low and the lenders flush with cash. This would then free up capital that could go to other borrowers to keep the economy moving.

Times were tough for many Americans following the Depression, and Roosevelt wanted to make it easier for middle- and low-income families to participate in the American dream of home ownership. (Keep in mind that home ownership is one of the great *trappings* of the American dream.) Fannie Mae seemed to solve this problem. But not quite.

Fannie Mae would fundamentally alter the workings of the financial system in which it operated.

Rather than making loans with the bank's capital only when they were confident the loan would be repaid, "entrepreneurial" lenders looking for a profit started to focus on giving loans that the government-sponsored entities would buy—with little, if any, attention to the quality of the borrower or their ability to repay the loan.

Securitization, to use the correct term, started in earnest with Fannie and continued with Freddie Mac's creation in 1970. But securitization wouldn't make its appearance onto center stage until the mortgage markets started to peak in 2007–2008. Only then could people finally appreciate the damage Fannie and Freddie had done to the system.

You see, while providing lenders with extra liquidity might keep the rates down, it ultimately boils down to throwing a big pile of cash into the mortgage market. And what happens when the amount of cash chasing houses is distorted and grows faster than it should?

You end up with an artificial rise in home prices. And you also have a large portion of the population assuming debt because money is easy and cheap to access.

From Fannie's inception in 1938 to 2006, home prices rose by 150 percent (adjusted for inflation). And mortgage debt continued to climb.

In 1949, mortgage debt was equal to 20 percent of total household income; by 1979, that number was 46 percent; and by 2001, it had reached 73 percent. Figure 1.1 shows the sense of the problem's scale in relation to the U.S. economy.

While this was an effective short-term response to keep homes affordable and within reach of Americans, it only succeeded in making home ownership more expensive for the average American (not to mention the American economy as a whole), thus making mortgage debt one of *the* chief contributors to the country's overwhelming indebtedness.

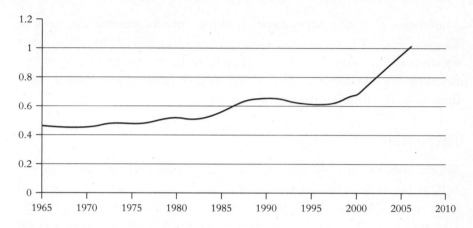

Figure 1.1 Mortgage Debt as Fraction of GDP

Source: www.econbrowser.com/archives/2008/01/mortgage_gdp.gif.

The Social Insurance Snowball—Sold as the Answer to Poverty

Another example of a short-term fix that has given us long-term problems takes us back again to the 1930s. Poverty rates for senior citizens started to exceed 50 percent. It was a political nightmare, and FDR was forced to take action. He implemented Social Security in 1935, as a means of social insurance to handle his—and the country's—current situation. It was sold as America's answer to poverty, even though it had to be clear from the beginning that the program would not be sustainable in the long term.

But, as with many other forms of entitlement, Social Security became ingrained in the public's expectations. Having contributed their own tax money to the program, Americans felt they had a right to benefit from what was originally intended to help one hard-luck generation bridge the gap in their personal finances. The problem snowballed over the years, with President Johnson revising the program and adding Medicare in 1965. By then it would have been political suicide for anyone to try to fix this unsustainable situation. Thus, Social Security has lived on years after it served its original purpose.

Today, Social Security and Medicare together add over $40 trillion in unfunded liabilities to the country's balance sheet. According to the

Washington Post, the two programs alone could consume upwards of 12 percent of America's gross domestic product (GDP) by 2024. That figure is about as much of the economy as the entire government represented just 100 years earlier, which is coincidentally within about a decade of the fund's anticipated insolvency.

Keeping up with the Joneses

When success spreads throughout the population, it's easy to get caught up in the material wealth accumulated from so many years of hard work. Buying your family's first house or your first car represents concrete proof that you've been successful; that you've done a good job. But by the 1950s and 1960s it became a matter of "keeping up with the neighbors," with housewives swearing under their breaths as they saw the Johnsons' new Chevrolet rolling down the street.

Even worse, the seeds of an entitlement culture that had been planted during the New Deal were nurtured alongside America's budding materialism.

Entitlement culture preyed on Americans' propensity for tolerance, generosity, and diversity, and subtly infiltrated an institution that for over 150 years had diligently and rigorously preserved the free enterprise of all American citizens.

And that's what really matters. It was not about the car or the house or the pension—it was about freedom. Freedom, above all else, to express yourself, to enjoy the fruits of your labor, and to be the captain of your own destiny. But such lofty ideals hardly translate smoothly into daily life, no matter how critical they may be.

Government Growth Spreads to the Judicial System

The 1950s are remembered as some of America's happiest years. And the 1960s are often remembered as a time of social reconstruction, of integration and civil rights. The 1960s were an emotionally charged decade that signaled a shift in what the masses thought about their government.

And it was a major shift—one where the U.S. government wasn't expected to *follow* the expectations and culture of the populace, but was now expected to *lead* it.

Tort Law is Born

After the war, the regulatory state was expanded, and courthouse doors were open to new claims that caused litigation to explode. Federal and state courts abandoned their historical view of hearing narrowly focused claims and expecting the plaintiff to be able to show proof of the damages. Plaintiff attorneys pushed hard for broader cases to be heard because this allowed them to profit handsomely.

The ongoing wave of new litigation was a change for the U.S. judicial system, and it resulted in an upsurge in the number of people attending law school. Lawyers were in greater demand, and the job was very lucrative.

The increase in litigation didn't only pack law schools and fill up courthouses. It had an impact on businesses and business owners, who had to deal with increased litigation from business partners, employees, vendors, customers, suppliers, and even the surrounding community. With more lawyers ready and willing to bring more cases to court, the direct costs associated with lawsuits increased. In many cases, the plaintiff wasn't sure to win, but many times the defendant would settle for a lesser amount out of court rather than spending more money to fight the claim.

Armed with the hope of quick settlements—where their case would not need to be proven in court—we have seen a rise in frivolous lawsuits targeting individuals, as well as companies, deemed wealthy enough to pay out.

Look where it has put us today.

In 2009, there were over 1.1 million lawyers—nearly half of all the lawyers in the world—at work in the United States of America. That's 1.1 million highly paid, often highly skilled legal professionals in need of constant work. And do they ever work! One study estimates that nearly 50,000 new lawsuits are filed in the United States *every single day*. Many of the lawsuits attack the wealth of unsuspecting victims.

It's critical to realize the costs of these suits. It is estimated that the U.S. legal system costs roughly a $252 billion (that's "billion" with a "b") a year, which is a fivefold increase since 1930. Rolled up in these costs are legal fees, court costs, judgments, and so on.

Currently, tort law costs total nearly 2 percent of the entire U.S. gross national product, the highest such figure among 12 industrialized

Western nations. And those costs are passed on to us. The costs for such litigation are passed directly on to consumers in the form of higher insurance rates and increased product prices.

A 2007 study by the Pacific Research Institute, a San Francisco "free-market" research group, alleges that the U.S. legal system imposes "a cost of $865 billion a year on the U.S. economy, or $9,800 a family." They claim that the costs associated with civil lawsuits and guarding against them is 27 times more than the federal government spends on homeland security, 30 times what the National Institutes of Health dedicates to biomedical research, and 13 times the amount the U.S. Department of Education spends to educate children.

In recent years, a proliferation of new laws and an unparalleled number of lawyers have begun to wear on the patience of American citizens and businesses. It's not hard to understand why, with recent cases like a group claiming an allergic reaction to Wi-Fi signals or a packaging company being sued for the unintended use of its product when a nightclub owner used polyethylene foam for soundproofing. The lure of easy money from quick settlements has become the norm.

The court systems were not alone in inspiring this revolution of abusive litigation. During this era, as you may recall, the executive and legislative branches were also hard at work expanding their roles and their rosters, and today's politicians have continued down this path. And with big-league benefits come big-league price tags.

THIRD GENERATION: 1970s–TODAY—PAYING THE PIPER IS OFTEN HARD

It wasn't long after the entitlements started flowing that the voting public started to indulge in "soak-the-rich" taxes in an effort to redistribute and best position the nation's wealth. This effectively brought about the demise of the first, most prodigious generation of the American economy and subsequently the second.

All the levels of government, which had once represented less than 15 percent of the national economy, began to blossom all at once. With new services and new benefits came new taxes. With new entitlements and types of mandatory government insurance came consistently rising rates.

But at least the taxes then were plainly visible on the surface. The more subversive element of the "buy now, pay later" era of politicians is that of inflation—the "stealth tax."

It's pretty simple, really.

It began in 1913, with the introduction of the United States' third central bank. (The first central bank failed, and the second was controversially dismantled by Andrew Jackson.) By setting benchmark interest rates, the Federal Reserve could affect growth in the money supply. It allowed the necessary control for the volatility of a *fiat* (debt-based) economic system, but it also incorporated an element of political expedience.

As we might expect, politicians promised increased spending, while cutting taxes. It was a great strategy that worked for a great many politicians. It allowed them to pay for their spending by increasing the money supply instead of collecting more taxes. They didn't have to "ask" the public for their money—they could just create more.

For years, all major countries used a fractional reserve system that limited how much money the government could print by how much gold or silver they held in reserve. Under this system, you could easily exchange U.S. dollars for physical gold at a local bank.

This system worked well for decades until the U.S. government had to find a way to pay for the ever-growing public debt as well as finance an unpopular Vietnam War.

In 1971, without enough gold to back the dollars needed to pay the current debts, the United States officially abandoned the link between gold and the U.S. dollar. A brave new world of free-floating currencies was ushered in and the rest of the world quickly created their own fiat money systems. Here at home, it gave the Federal Reserve the ability to inflate or deflate the money supply as it saw fit.

Total Amount of Federal Spending per Family:
More Spending = More Inflation

The strength of the "stealth" tax is in the fact that most people don't understand purchasing power and how quickly you can lose it in a fiat economy.

It's simple, really. An inflation rate of 25 percent means that for every dollar you have, there's now $1.25 in the economy, and prices will adjust accordingly. That $1 pretzel will now cost $1.25, whether you have that extra quarter in your pocket or not. Gradually, this theft of purchasing power will diminish the power of your savings and income, unless they can keep up with the rate of inflation.

The inflation rate is marginal most of the time, often 2 to 5 percent or less. But it builds up over time.

Figure 1.2 shows the declining purchasing power of the dollar in the twentieth century. By 2001, the amount of goods you could buy with a dollar were about as same as the amount you could've bought with four cents at the beginning of the century. Or think of it like this: you could have bought a basket of assorted goods for $1 back in 1913. By 2001, that same basket cost you $25.

Unraveling the stealth tax takes you back to the days when a movie cost a nickel or a dime, a soda or an ice cream would set you back about as much, and cigars went for 50 cents.

Granted, some of this growth is justified.

Just like everything else, populations and wages have increased significantly. Our economy has become more robust, and consumer

Figure 1.2 Purchasing Power of the Federal Reserve Note in 1913 Dollars

Source: www.norfed.org/graphics/home/purchasepower.jpg.

goods more abundant. Thus, some of the inflation is absorbed by these increases.

But for the last decade, that simply hasn't been the case.

Mortgaging America's Future (and the Future of Your Wealth)

Just like any other top executive, the politicians in Washington and the White House have faced decades of extreme pressure to generate short-term results.

And they succeeded—in the short term.

The third generation's ability to create wealth has been eroded. Thanks in great part to the bursting of two separate bubbles—the technology bubble of 2000 and, more recently, the housing bubble— plus the government's growing drag on the economy, recent data indicates that there was zero net job creation in the first decade of the twenty-first century. The past decade also saw household net worth drop by 5 percent, compared to increases of 44 percent in the 1960s and 58 percent in the 1990s.

As Ronald Reagan once said, "the nine most terrifying words in the English language are: I'm from the government and I'm here to help." Looking back, it's no surprise that his words met with such uproarious applause. Today, especially, they ring true.

Since 1999, the government has come to "help" in a big way, adding employees at a rate 40 percent faster than the rate of population growth. And this wasn't a new trend, not by any means.

As you can see in Figure 1.3, the government grew four times faster than the economy for most of the twentieth century and into the twenty-first.

What a racket.

The average government salary is around $75,000 in recent years, compared to an average of $45,000 in the private sector. According to a *USA Today* article from 2008, federal employees making salaries of $100,000 or more jumped from 14 percent to 19 percent during the recession's first 18 months—and that's before overtime pay and bonuses are counted. So while hundreds of thousands of Americans were losing their jobs and their homes, a full 5 percent of federal employees made the leap into a six-figure annual salary. By 2008,

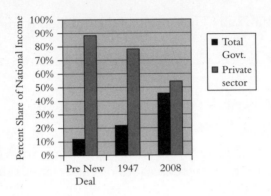

Figure 1.3 Government (federal + state + local) Grows Four Times Faster than Economy—Depressing Private Sector's Share

Source: Grandfather Economic Report (http://mwhodges.home.att.net/); data: Bureau of Economic Analysis.

the government's once-tiny slice had grown into 45 percent of the national economy.

And it shows no signs of slowing down.

In the Bureau of Labor Statistics' projections for 2008–2018, several categories of government jobs (local government, teachers, etc.) are featured prominently among the fastest-growing industries and occupations in America. Local government payrolls, for example, are expected to grow over 8 percent during that period, while enduring the first major wave of Baby Boomer retirements. These retirees will soon begin to cash in on the bulk of their government entitlements, putting unprecedented stress on everything from Social Security to Medicare and government pension programs.

Meanwhile, in the past two decades another opposite trend has manifested in the private workforce.

For most of the twentieth century, with home prices rising, taxes consuming an average of 40 percent of income, and unions beginning to dominate many traditional industries, American workers demanded more in wages. They demanded more benefits. Attorneys assaulted employers from another angle with a host of lawsuits.

Private business in America became a much more bothersome affair than it had once been. Over time, thanks to the power

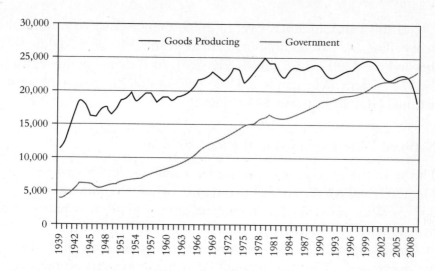

Figure 1.4 Goods Producing vs. Government Payrolls
Source: U.S. Department of Labor.

and speed of technology, production went abroad—Japanese motorcycles, Chinese televisions and toys, and so on. America's economy, increasingly dominated by the service sector, found itself with less and less of a concrete industrial infrastructure to fall back on.

In January 2010, in the wake of so many private-sector layoffs and government hirings, the scales finally tipped, and as you can see in Figure 1.4, America's labor force became dominated by government employees.

A "Debt-aholic" Government

The legacy of the U.S. federal government is a costly one. What you might not expect is just *how* costly.

If every man, woman, and child in America were asked to pay their share of the U.S. national debt tomorrow, they'd all need to find over $39,000 *each*. Assume they all paid in $1 bills (because why not), and you'd have roughly four stacks of $1 bills, touching the Earth on one side and the moon on the other.

You don't have to search very far for the trail of a debt-fiend government.

Just this past Christmas Eve, in 2009, Congress voted to raise the debt ceiling and extend unlimited aid to Fannie Mae and Freddie Mac (beyond the $200 billion already pledged). At the time of this writing, the U.S. federal debt stands at $12.1 trillion dollars, against an annual national GDP of just over $14 trillion.

National Debt Exploded in the Past 20 Years

Throw in the government's unfunded liabilities, like Social Security, Medicare, and Medicaid, and that number rises well above $54 trillion dollars. With just over $14 trillion in annual GDP, it is pretty clear that we have overstretched a little (see Figures 1.5 and 1.6).

To be sure, interest rates on long-term debt are some of the lowest we've ever seen. The government's financing costs aren't prohibitive—at least not yet. And as for the $54 trillion in unfunded liabilities, well, those aren't all due this year. That's the total projected amount of outlays for Social Security and Medicare over an extended period of time.

But it takes a bit of a thinker to realize the real implications of such an astronomical number. Namely, there's someone out there who owns $39,000 in debt for every American man, woman, and child. Now more than ever the person holding our debt is not one of us.

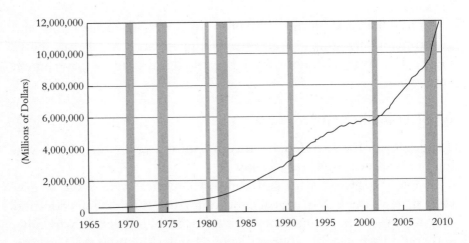

Figure 1.5 Federal Government Debt: Total Public Debt

Note: Shaded areas indicate U.S. recessions.

Source: U.S. Department of Treasury, Financial Management Service; 2009 research.stlouisfed.org.

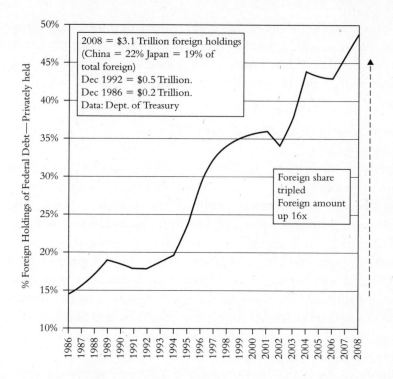

The inset box reads:

2008 = $3.1 Trillion foreign holdings
(China = 22% Japan = 19% of
total foreign)
Dec 1992 = $0.5 Trillion.
Dec 1986 = $0.2 Trillion.
Data: Dept. of Treasury

Foreign share
tripled
Foreign amount
up 16x

Y-axis: % Foreign Holdings of Federal Debt—Privately held

Figure 1.6 Foreign Holdings of Federal Government T-Bill and T-Bond Debt (held by "public")
Source: Grandfather Economic Report, http://mwhodges.home.att.net.

Since the mid-1980s, just as the U.S. debt was passing a historic landmark of $2 trillion dollars, the share of debt owned by foreign nations has tripled. The overall dollar amount they control has exploded—16 times the amount foreign nations controlled in 1986. Currently, the top five foreign holders of our debt include China, Japan, the United Kingdom, oil exporters (countries in OPEC like Iran, Iraq, Kuwait, Libya, Nigeria, Saudi Arabia, and Venezuela), and Caribbean banking centers including Bermuda and the Bahamas.

How exactly will this affect the outcome of the next few decades? Perhaps nothing will come from more and more foreign nations owning U.S. debt. However, there is a risk that those holding our debt may want to have a say in our government policies and practices, especially if they impact any of the involved nations. With China holding the largest foreign share of U.S. debt, their opinions may impact the U.S. government's decision to implement protectionist steel tariffs. It's possible that the United States could lose its autonomy to make the necessary decisions to revive its economy.

NEARING THE BOILING POINT

This is very likely to bring about a reckoning day for all levels of government in the United States—probably nothing catastrophic, much more like an uncomfortable readjustment in all likelihood. The state will survive. However, personal fortunes may not be so lucky.

State, local, and municipal governments, facing their own hiring expectations and pension obligations, will soon be prominent default risks. Taxes will no longer be able to cover pension payouts and short-term obligations. They will have two alternatives: to endure a rash of defaults and a spike in rates or seek a federal bailout. Like the financial system, they'll likely see a series of bailouts and initiatives aimed at helping maintain "liquidity."

Underneath it all, the U.S. federal government is making a major long-term play. They're sacrificing the value of the U.S. dollar—or, at the very least, risking it—to smooth over the shock from the massive global transfer of wealth that's once again under way.

In 1873, that shift brought with it the Long Depression, a period lasting over six years. But the U.S. economy would stumble for decades, experiencing a host of economic setbacks from 1873 to 1901. Also, keep in mind what the global backlash was like for Hungary—now considered an emerging market—and Germany, which has just recently become reinvigorated in the past decade after the struggles of reunification.

But this time around, the world is in a unique position.

For the first time in history, we're undergoing a global economic crisis without a single currency backed by anything other than debt. The days of the gold-backed currencies are long gone. So we can expect that policymakers will, without a doubt, make unprecedented use of their powers (and their printing presses) to favor their people.

Indeed, governments throughout the world are enacting bailouts, stimulus, and quantitative easing. These practices and their euphemisms are likely to stay with us for several years, or until this crisis of debt and value that is still in the works comes to a head. One way or another, we believe it's highly likely that a great many American savers, investors, and wealthy individuals could face a serious "rude awakening" in the relatively near future.

We feel compelled to remind you at this point: these aren't doomsday scenarios we've been talking about.

The projections we've shown you have largely been based on government-prepared data, coming from some relatively trustworthy sources such as the Congressional Budget Office. Looking to the same individuals and think tanks that predicted the largely unforeseen subprime crisis, we hear much more startling projections—those of volatility, of record defaults, and the potential for hyperinflation.

WITH CRISIS COMES OPPORTUNITY

Regardless which of these futures sounds the most reasonable to you, a few things are clear.

Americans will need more proactive protection for their wealth, more forethought and insight than ever before. The resources are currently at your fingertips, but the challenge is formidable. You'll need protection from frivolous lawsuits. You'll need protection from the continuing erosion of the value of the U.S. dollar, thanks to federal spending and government stealth. You'll need protection from a rapidly growing government that will change the U.S. economy and marketplace, which entails a *new* kind of diversification.

America's prospects might indeed look bleak depending on where you stand. But with each crisis comes opportunity; however, this time you may not find opportunity at home.

FINDING THE NEW LAND OF OPPORTUNITY AND SAFETY

The financial landscape is changing. While exciting developments and investment breakthroughs are still happening each day, they are happening more and more frequently on non-U.S. shores.

Billions of people will wake each morning to face new challenges and take new risks. It's hard to say which ventures will prove successful—which companies will create the next "big" opportunity—but some things are certain.

The *Les Trente Glorieuses* are over. And the days of a Chevy in every driveway have passed; it's more likely to be a Kia or a Honda. We have entered a decade where economic and market volatility will be the norm, where threats to personal wealth will continue to proliferate, and U.S. government expansion will continue on a course like no other time in history. It also means that for many of us the traditional investment method of American stocks and bonds will simply not suffice. If we do not look beyond our borders, we will miss out on the next decade of revolutionary investment growth, and in doing so, we'll put our hard-earned capital at risk.

CHAPTER 2

PASSING THE WEALTH BATON

Building a Sustainable Investment and Savings Plan to Ensure a Solid Financial Future

So how do the twenty-first century saver and investor respond to all the issues and demands of a changing investment landscape?

Well, as you can likely already tell, it's going to take something different. And as you to add it all up, it starts to look like a tall order. . . .

Your first reaction might be to pack up the house, rent a moving truck, and say good-bye to the United States. And while that's an option, it's probably not realistic. You have family, friends, possibly even a business here at home, and you shouldn't give that up. You do not need to jump ship, but you do need to take steps to buffer the impact the coming global power shift will have on your financial future.

As discussed earlier, the costs of mounting federal debt, endless entitlement obligations, stealth taxes, outrageous lawsuits, and emerging economies all point toward an event horizon in which America's financial future is completely uncertain.

If each of these things had happened one at a time, things might not seem so dire. However, the reality is that a decades-long transition—one where financial control is passed across oceans and borders to a younger, hungrier economy—is already well under way.

If you're trying to create a long-term investment strategy in this climate, there are four steps you should take in order to build an investment and savings plan based on the current state of affairs:

Step 1. First, you'll need protection from a rapidly growing government that will change the U.S. economy and marketplace, which entails a *new* kind of diversification.

Step 2. Second, you'll need protection from the continuing erosion of the value of the U.S. dollar, thanks to federal spending and government stealth.

Step 3. Third, you'll need protection from frivolous lawsuits, which will continue to explode as those with deep pockets are sought out as targets.

Step 4. Finally, all this saving and investing is a smart move only if your ultimate goal is to be able to benefit from it in the future or make sure that the people you care about benefit after you're gone. So proper estate planning is a must.

We will start with importance of diversifying your investments across the global markets and why this will continue to rise in importance in the coming years.

STEP 1: FOR WORLD-CLASS INVESTMENT RETURNS, YOU NEED WORLD-CLASS INVESTMENTS—THE IMPORTANCE OF GLOBAL MARKETS IN THE TWENTY-FIRST CENTURY

The start of our current financial crisis happened on a fateful summer afternoon, June 22, 2007. That afternoon, Bear Stearns—the fast-growing star of the global investment banking business—announced that it would need to take action and bail out two of its hedge funds due to deteriorating subprime investments.

It didn't seem like a major event.

Few outside of the financial sector even took notice. Indeed, even today you may not remember the event, even though it was ostensibly the "canary in the coal mine" for the titans of global banking.

Likewise, another minor story came across the wire just six days later, one with far larger implications. It was the *Financial Express*, with a story from New Delhi, proudly declaring that India was home to 1 million millionaires. The country's young population of millionaires was growing at a startling rate of 20 percent a year.

These two announcements, released just days apart from one another, were the bellwethers of the trend we discussed in the first chapter—a trend that's got you and your financial future caught right in the middle. In the span of little more than a week, the "baton" signifying growing private wealth quietly passed from America to a handful of others.

The "American" Dream Finds a New Home

India might be at the head of the pack, but by no means are they alone. . . .

In China, net household wealth nearly tripled from $1.3 trillion to $3.4 trillion in three short years, between 2004 and 2007. In November 2009, the number of Chinese millionaires jumped to over 450,000. Yet that number is expected to nearly double in the next 15 years, reaching 788,000 by 2023. Similar trends are under way in other emerging markets, specifically Russia and Brazil.

The once-proud capital of the former communist empire, Moscow, is now home to more billionaires than New York. Over 30 of the world's few hundred billionaires call South America home.

In fact, just since 2001—a decade that would see zero net job creation in the United States and a first-ever decline in household wealth—the pace of entrepreneurs crossing the million-dollar mark has exploded in the other nations, so much so that they have even begun to dominate the *Forbes* list of the world's 100 richest billionaires (see Figure 2.1).

And it's important to stress that this is real wealth creation.

These emerging-market millionaires haven't built "bubble fortunes" of stock market or real estate wealth that comes crashing down every time the market panics.

Instead, many of these new global millionaires have built their wealth the old-fashioned way—through innovation, determination, and brute force of will. They've built and refined their local markets, offered new products at reasonable prices in domestic markets, and

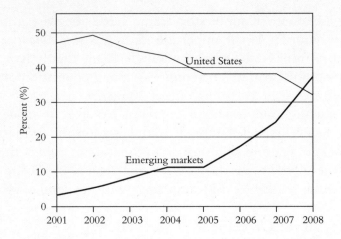

Figure 2.1 World's 100 Richest Billionaires; Percent in U.S. vs. Emerging Markets 2001–2008
Source: Forbes.

embraced the type of qualities that were once the trademark of the American entrepreneurs.

Yet, today, many people still believe that America is the economic and political center of the world while the rest of the globe quietly continues to exist in the background. This is a dangerously out-of-date view of America's position in the world, and it can be costly to investors who choose to believe it. The savvy saver and investor must be aware of what's developing and be able to capitalize on investment opportunities wherever they may arise.

The harsh truth is the dream of going from rags to riches due to ingenuity, skill, and hard work in a land fertile with opportunity is no longer the American dream. That dream is now coming to life in countries far away from Wall Street, or downtown Detroit, or the stagnant halls of the Capitol building in Washington, D.C.

The American Dream: Gone Global

While America's "third generation" was busy divvying up the spoils of over a century of innovation and economic success, a new, hungry, first generation was being born in the corners of the globe.

Ravaged by years of war, living at the far reaches of the global political scene, they were born in Vietnam, Singapore, and India. They were born in Brazil and China and Eastern Europe. And for the most part, they were born in or surrounded by abject poverty.

And more than any past generation, it was virtually impossible for them to escape news of their neighbor's wealth. New American inventions spread news of the American dream faster than ever. And their effects were dazzling upon the world's people, who were for the most part scarcely familiar with innovations of the nineteenth century, let alone the twentieth.

Given the chance, the deck was obviously stacked in their favor.

Unlike their counterparts in the Western world, the entrepreneurs of the emerging market weren't born into wealth. They weren't transfixed on government entitlements or welfare initiatives. To the contrary, they more often had a healthy loathing of government and the impact it had on the populace in recent years.

So they were hungry not only to escape poverty, but to provide their countrymen with a better life, with more opportunities. For decades they watched and listened on television and radio as American innovators time and time again demonstrated man's power to transform the world around him. They saw a man light up the night with electricity. They saw an American walking on the face of the moon. And they watched as American cars, computers, and the Internet all flooded their country and changed life in their own country. Inspired, they looked to their own country, to its oft-battered political and financial institutions, and they began to make transformations of their own.

Many from this generation were born into the shells of failed states, where the promises of communism or fascism had in time failed to keep up with the needs of the populace. As Benjamin Franklin would have it, they had traded freedom for safety, and somehow lost both in the process. But a shift in ideology is already well under way.

Globalizing the Economy—Americanizing at Home

Like the immigrants who landed on America's shore and gave birth to the original dream, these new entrepreneurs are ready to explore the alternatives. They are thirsty for growth, thirsty for a better life for themselves and their people. Their own personal experience extolled the hazards of too much government, of planned economies and over-whelming bureaucracy.

They're not fleeing to a "clean slate" country across the ocean. Instead, these countries are filled with native populations, native cultures, and native customs. Their political systems often arise from such native customs, rather than being based on the prevailing eighteenth-century schools of philosophy that played such a large role in the founding ideology of the United States.

Instead, the world's emerging markets would have to "reverse-engineer" the successes Western capitalism enjoyed in the twentieth century. They would have to somehow integrate America's winning "free enterprise" ideology with a more familiar, more comfortable set of laws and doctrines. And in many cases, they needed to achieve a great deal of economic growth without upsetting their own sensitive balance of power.

Nowhere was this more difficult than in China, where the ideology and the single-party political institution were generally accepted to be the diametric opposite of a free-enterprise society.

For years, China has lacked the legal infrastructure to *protect* and maintain free enterprise. Foreign investors weren't exactly tripping over themselves to invest in a country without patent laws. But by the early 1990s the government had a handle on the necessary trans-formations: less red tape, less bureaucracy, lower taxes. The "Special Economic Zones" (SEZs) that were created in 1978, when China started to allow foreign investments in certain regions of the country, finally started to flourish.

These SEZs quickly became hotbeds for economic growth, with mammoth industrial complexes sprouting up as far as the eye could see. The level of wages, the promise of subsidies and returns, and the overwhelming demand for cheap goods all aligned and China's economy exploded (see Figure 2.2).

And look at China today. It's hard to find a product that doesn't have a "Made in China" imprint on it somewhere. And as the world's manu-facturer, China's role in the world economy has changed dramatically.

We won't deny that China's growth and their fiscal policies have possibly created a few rather serious bubbles in the Chinese stock market as well as in real estate. Right now, China faces a lot

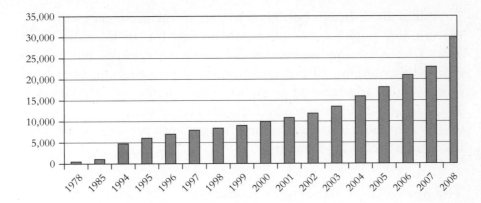

Figure 2.2 China's Economy: 35 Times Growth in 20 Years of Liberalization

Note: Gross domestic product (GDP): billion RMB.
Sources: National Bureau of Statistics of China, www.stats.gov.cn/tjsj/ndsj/2008/indexch.htm; www.stats.gov.cn/tjgb/ndtjgb/qgndtjgb/t20090226_402540710.htm (accessed 29 May 2009).

of "ifs." *If* foreign investors turn 180 degrees . . . *if* the Chinese real estate bubble bursts . . . *if* consumer demand continues to disappoint—any of these calamities could cause significant *short-term* pain in the Chinese economy. But at the end of the day, China has trillions of dollars in currency reserves, while America has $12 trillion in national debt (and counting). Thanks to the progress of economic liberalization and the gradual benefits it brings, China's future is much brighter.

Of course, China is not alone. . . .

In the 1980s, the Chilean government brought in the "Chicago Boys," a team of economists educated at the University of Chicago, and heavily influenced by the writings of Milton Friedman. In the 1990s, Chile saw robust economic growth, with 1 million Chileans rising above the poverty line. In that time, stocks took off, rising by 1,725 percent.

After the fall of the Soviet Union, in 1993, Poland began a radical wave of privatization. In that single year, the stock market soared by over 1,100 percent. And in 2002, eastern Europe began a new round of economic reform in preparation for joining the European Union. Like clockwork, economies grew at record levels and markets soared. Poland's stock market rose by over 550 percent, the Czech Republic's by 1,391 percent, and Hungary's by over 500 percent.

Also in 2002, Inacio Lula Da Silva ran for the presidency of Brazil. He ran as a populist, but ultimately turned out to be more practical. That is, he implemented social safety net reforms, but he also reduced the amount of red tape, increased privatization, liberalized foreign trade, and reduced taxes. The stock market rose 130 percent in a year, and 2,000 percent over the next seven years.

But economic liberalization and hungry entrepreneurs alone don't make for a successful economy.

The Key to Understanding Economies in the Long Haul

It's true that the world's rapidly growing countries are far less developed and regulated. An entrepreneur in the United States has to comply with a mountain of regulations, obtaining permits, licenses, insurance, even costly legal advice just to get a business started. And if there's any profit or fun left in the business after that, you've still got to wrestle with the fear of being sued or violating some unknown set of rules or regulations. The barrier for entry is significantly lower in other countries, meaning you don't often need much more than a good idea, a little money, and some willpower to make something happen. But how successful a country will be depends not only on the ambition of their people and the country's economic policies, but also on their demographics.

Demographics are important when it comes to looking at a country for future investment. In case you're not familiar with it, demographic investing is the practice of basing your decisions on the trending age of a country's population and the demands that will follow that age. It can produce impressive long-term returns if done right.

Demographic investing can also help you avoid the obvious hazards. Let's look at two major nations: Japan and the United States.

Back in 1950, Japan's population, as seen on the left side of Figure 2.3, looks very much like a pyramid. It had a hefty base skewed toward an explosively large younger generation. In 2007, as the country continued to age and develop, the demographics were more evenly distributed between all the age groups. The bulk of the Japanese population fell right in a sweet spot—ages 20 to 60—when people are at the peak of consuming and producing.

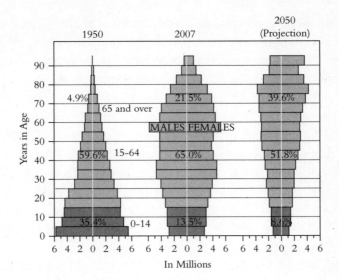

Figure 2.3 Japan's Demographic Changes
Sources: Japan Statistics Bureau, MIC; Ministry of Health, Labour and Welfare.

But as you can see from the forecast for 2050, Japan's future is . . . well, it's old. And that wobbly graph has major implications for the country. As people get older, they stop bringing in income. Their consumption slows down, and their rate of savings generally reverses as they begin to live off the savings they accumulated during their primary working years.

Retirement itself isn't a problem for an economy. But when it happens on a massive scale, it can become disastrous. You see, in 1990, at the beginning of the country's first lost decade, Japan's elderly made up 19 percent of the total population. The waning consumption of the retired elderly, combined with their draw-downs from social programs, has no doubt contributed to the country's current quagmire, which the United States is now closely mirroring.

As a quick aside, we should point out that the United States is following the same path that Japan has already traveled in more ways than one. Japan faced the burst of a real estate bubble in the late 1980s, resulting in bank failures and write-offs for more than a decade afterwards.

The Japanese government responded by slashing interest rates, leading to a deflationary spiral that has seen its stock market, the Nikkei, stuck down over 70 percent from its peak, reflecting nearly two decades of economic stagnation (see Figure 2.4).

Today, America finds itself on the edge of the same precipice. Facing our own Lost Decade, the elderly comprised roughly the same percentage (20 percent) of the American population in 2009.

Indeed, if you look at Figure 2.5, you will see that American workforce demographics are following Japan as well. To be sure, these are two different countries comprised of hundreds of millions of people. But thanks to similar demographics, the extent of each country's welfare state and entitlement systems, and current economic climate, we can certainly expect to see some of the same macroeconomic trends on our side of the Pacific.

Meanwhile, in emerging countries like Brazil, for example, less than 7 percent of the country's population is over 65 years of age. The majority of their population is currently 24 years of age and younger. That means that despite all the new emerging-market millionaires,

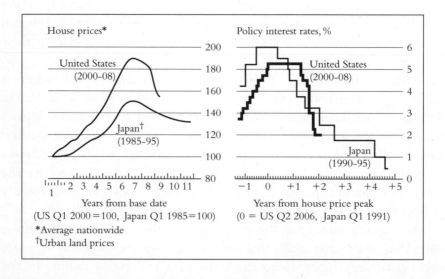

Figure 2.4 Japan and the United States—A Tale of Two Bubbles

Sources: S&P/Case-Shiller; Japan Real Estate Institute; Thomson Datastream.

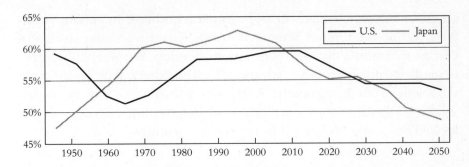

Figure 2.5 Proportion of Working-Age Population in United States and Japan

some 20 percent of the country is just now entering the workforce, generating income, savings, consumption—forming new economic relationships and new channels for profit. Likewise, 40 percent of the Indian population (or about 400 million out of a billion people) are under the age of 20.

China, Indonesia, and Pakistan all have populations where the median age is in the low 20s. These nations have people as another valuable resource, which will help their nations grow. Their young people will become inventors and business owners.

With newly liberalized economies, business-friendly regulatory environments, and an array of favorable demographics, with billions of people just now coming into their heyday of spending and consumption—these are all factors favoring emerging-market growth in the long term.

And with so much room to innovate, expand, and enrich the economy, the world's emerging markets will be rife with investing opportunities for foreigners like you. Indeed, these countries will need massive amounts of foreign direct investment to keep modernizing and building the economy. You've got to remember, like we said at the beginning of this section, many of these countries are lacking innovations of the twentieth century. So there's more than enough opportunity—opportunities such as cell phone technology in Africa or affordable pharmaceuticals in India.

As the "American" dream continues to expand and develop, it will usher in a new level of prosperity to any nation that allows its citizens to embrace it. Job creation, true economic growth, innovations, and scientific breakthroughs will all be easier to achieve in certain countries. While the United States will struggle in the coming years, it is certain that humanity will continue to develop, explore, and create. Regardless of where these advances happen, there will be investors who will profit handsomely. And even a select few will build vast wealth all because they correctly read the writing on the wall and looked beyond their home borders for opportunity.

Profiting from the "New" First Generation

Today, there is a new first generation changing their country's economy and creating industries that significantly impact the world markets. It shouldn't take much to convince for an investor to realize that he needs to move part of his wealth so that he can participate in all of this global growth.

While the United States has the world's largest securities markets, more than 50 percent of the world's stock investment opportunities are in other countries. As we have already discussed, many of these countries are growing much faster than the United States. In fact, the majority of the world's biggest companies in major industries trade on non-U.S. markets, including:

- Nine of the ten largest mining companies
- Eight of the ten largest electronic equipment companies
- Seven of the ten largest car manufacturers
- Seven of the ten largest telecommunications companies

As a global twenty-first-century investor, you have a wide choice among various financial products to access international opportunities from a distance, including:

- Global stocks
- Global bonds
- Foreign currencies
- Global exchange-traded funds
- Global hedge funds
- Managed futures
- Global investment trusts

However, while the tools exist to give you access, the difficulty—and sometimes impossibility—of accessing these international investments is a harsh reality. More and more countries are making a concerted effort to force their citizens and residents to keep their money in their home country. The United States is one such country.

Americans from all walks of life are finding it difficult to open investment accounts overseas, which are required to truly participate in the foreign markets because the U.S. government has placed burdensome demands on offshore banks and money managers. Many large banks and international firms that serve clients from all major countries are now refusing to accept American clients because they fear legal entanglements with the U.S. authorities.

The United States has introduced a number of regulations that may adversely impact foreign financial institutions, even though these companies do not operate on U.S. soil. For many of these institutions it has not only become very costly to be compliant with the American laws, but impossible for them to do so without violating domestic laws in the country where they operate. So your ability to even open a foreign bank account to gain access to the world's investments has become a much more time-consuming task.

Even if you successfully locate a foreign bank that's willing to work with you, the real challenge still remains: *how* do you get invested? One of the easiest and potentially most lucrative ways to access international and emerging markets is through global mutual funds.

But, inevitably, you'll discover that most mutual funds, alternative investments (hedge funds), and other investment companies won't accept you as an investor for the simple reason that they don't want to get entangled with the U.S. authorities, including the Securities and Exchange Commission (SEC), Internal Revenue Service (IRS), and other U.S. financial regulatory bodies. Thus, your nationality alone will exclude you from being able to invest.

Here in the United States it is almost impossible for an investor to purchase international mutual fund shares in these lucrative markets without paying onerous taxes. Plus, the SEC prohibits offshore or non-U.S. registered funds from soliciting U.S. investors. So there's a very good chance you would never hear even hear about these funds.

In theory, this is to protect U.S. investors from unscrupulous and unregulated investments. But a number of very good offshore fund companies out there aren't registered with the SEC, simply because they do not want to be bothered with all of the paperwork and filing requirements of the SEC (and IRS), just so they can market their funds in the United States.

As a result, the American investor gets short-changed. You can't invest in the best possible investments. Instead, you're stuck with what's left on the investment menu based on your nationality, some of which may or may not be suitable or profitable.

Why IRAs and 401(k)s Simply Are Not Enough

Most American families have the bulk of their investable assets in some type of retirement plan. So the average investor might have a little international exposure to lucrative emerging markets or European investments through an individual retirement account (IRA) or 401(k).

In general, there are on average eight investment options available within most 401(k) plans. These traditional options allow you to diversify your portfolio into high-risk and low-risk investments that have been selected by the investment company that manages the overall plan, such as Fidelity, Pension, or Merrill Lynch. However, only one of these options offers you the opportunity to invest in international funds.

And more often than not, you will be limited to only a few funds at best. While you might be able to select a fund that tracks the performance of European Union stock markets, you would not be able to pinpoint a specific company, fund, or sector in that market. You would be locked out from having the ability to invest in a Turkish lira bond, or a German steel company, or an up-and-coming Israeli battery technology company.

Also, most 401(k) plans offer access only to international funds that meet the investment strategies and beliefs of their U.S.-based advisers. They select the funds they believe will do well; however, their view of the long-term outlook may not match yours. Nor will your plan give you the ability to invest in specific long-term trends. For example, if you have a long-term investment horizon, why not create an investment strategy that invests in the prevailing demographic trends of emerging markets? For example, let's take India. You could invest in key Indian banking stocks just as the youth in India enter their prime years of consumption. As they're starting to buy houses and cars, save, and invest, you're invested in a select handful of India's finest banks. Additionally, as they grow older, you shift your funds into—again—a select handful of health care stocks, catching the rising demand of an aging population.

Without direct access to international markets and international investment managers, you aren't just at risk of missing long-term trends. You can also miss out on the opportunity to have your money put to work in some amazing companies around the global. For example, we bet few of you have ever heard of Li Ning Company Limited.

Li Ning is China's version of the sportswear industry giant Nike. The company markets, researches and develops, designs, manufactures, distributes, and retails products including footwear, apparel, accessories, and equipment for sport and leisure uses just like Nike.

The company trades on the Hong Kong Stock Exchange, and its growth has been astounding, seeing revenues more than double between 2006 and 2008, rising to $892 million. Li Ning bought a major sponsorship in the 2008 Beijing Olympics and sponsors several teams in China, as well as Spain and Sweden. However, less than 1 percent of the company's revenue is generated outside of China.

But the average American investor probably hasn't heard of this company and its astounding growth; instead, they are investing in the likes of large-cap, slow-growth Goliath Nike. As a younger, growth-oriented company, Li Ning has trounced Nike in every major financial category in the past six years. In fact, from 2004 to 2009, while Nike has seen a 100 percent increase in stock price, Li Ning has increased 1,000 percent (see Figure 2.6).

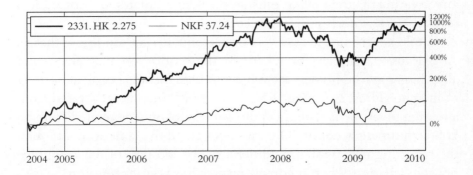

Figure 2.6   Li Ning Growing Leaps and Bounds Compared to Nike
Source: Yahoo Finance.

These types of opportunities, and many thousands more like them, are available if you know where to find them, but it's critical that you know the best way to access them.

Understanding the U.S. Tax Requirements is Critical

Once you decide to move a portion of your assets out of the United States and invest in opportunities abroad, you must look for ways do so in a tax-efficient manner, or you could be faced with some deal-breaking tax consequences.

No doubt, we all need to pay our due taxes to keep the country going. But that's not the problem. The problem is that most governments keep spending and promising far too much for the national checkbook to back up. The U.S. government isn't alone in building a mountain of national debt—but don't worry. They've got a solution for that. Many will turn to inflating their debt, or they will create new taxes in order to make up for the shortfalls between their promises and reality. As a result, the tax burden becomes increasingly heavy for society's more successful members.

But, to be clear, there are no completely tax-free ways to invest. Should you decide to internationalize your investment portfolio by investing with a foreign bank or working with an international money manager, you will not save anything with regard to U.S. taxes. This is important to point out because in our travels, as recently as only a few months ago, we continue to meet people who wrongly believe that any investments they make outside the United States are not subject to U.S. taxes. This is simply not correct.

While we are not tax lawyers or accountants, we do know that all Americans—regardless of where in the world you may live—and all U.S. green card holders are subject to U.S. income tax on all sources of income. Thus, as far the IRS is concerned, income generated from a foreign investment account is the same as income generated from an U.S. investment account. They are both taxed the same way, although the reporting may be slightly different. The location of the account is not what matters when it comes to taxes. It's your citizenship.

So while tax will play a role in any investments you make as an American, it is important for you to understand that the U.S.

government has a host of rules and regulations surrounding international investments and specifically how Americans can compliantly access them. Some are more tax favorable than others.

For successful investors to stay ahead in the twenty-first century, they will need to figure out a way to minimize the taxes that they pay. Again, to be clear, we are not talking about avoiding your required tax bill. But why pay more than is required? Your wealth means more to you than just a tax contribution to fund some Washington politician's dreams of a better world.

The way in which your international investments are taxed varies based on how you hold those investments. Here, we will briefly cover the most common ways, and we will highlight a potential tax trap you could fall into if you aren't careful. (*Note*: We are discussing only the tax treatment of the investments and not the U.S. reporting requirements.)

Should you decide to invest in foreign stocks, bonds, or currencies through a foreign bank, any investment gains that may be realized will be treated the same as domestic investment gains. This means that your foreign-derived profits—whether they come from the appreciation of the investment or an appreciation in a foreign currency, or both—will be subject to capital gains. Capital gains are taxed differently depending on whether your investment is considered a long-term or a short-term investment.

The short-term holding period is one year or less, and short-term capital gains are taxed at ordinary income tax rates. The long-term holding period is more than one year and the current long-term tax rate for most investors is 15 percent. For most investors this is customary and straightforward.

The situations become trickier when it comes to foreign mutual funds or hedge funds. These types of investments are very common in the international world. However, for American investors, these types of funds are subject to very unfavorable taxation due to passive foreign investment company (PFIC) rules (Appendix B-1). Foreign mutual funds are treated as PFICs under the Internal Revenue Code. It's important that you be aware of this distinction because the tax penalties can be quite stiff.

Technically speaking, a PFIC is any foreign company that derives at least 75 percent of its gross income from passive activities or that derives passive income from at least 50 percent of its assets. Nearly all of the income of a mutual fund is generally passive income. So, according to the IRS's definition, nearly all foreign mutual funds are PFICs.

Originally conceived years ago to be a deterrent to tax avoidance, the consequences for a U.S. resident or citizen owning a share in a PFIC are rather severe. Basically, it turns capital gains tax into ordinary income tax, eating away a huge portion of your investment growth before you can reinvest it (more on this in a moment). Distributions of fund shares deemed to be from prior years' earnings of the PFIC may be taxed at the highest rate for ordinary income in each prior year, and there may even be an interest charge on the deferred distribution. It is possible for PFICs to be taxed up to 48 percent in some cases.

In addition to the extremely unfavorable tax situation, each PFIC investor is confronted with a complicated reporting responsibility each and every year. The burden is so complicated, in fact, that most funds cannot and will not provide you with the information that you need for compliant IRS reporting. Given the number and complexity of these rules—and the outrageous tax levels involved—it is almost always advisable to avoid investment in a PFIC.

Using a foreign company as a holding structure to access the international investment universe may confront you with the controlled foreign corporation (CFC) rules (Appendix B-2). Under U.S. law, a foreign corporation is considered a CFC if at least 50 percent of either the total voting power or total value of the stock of the foreign corporation is owned by a U.S. persons, each of whom owns at least 10 percent of the voting power of the corporation.

With a CFC the shareholders are taxed on their share of the corporation whether or not the income in the company is distributed. This often includes interest, dividends, rents, royalties, and business income derived from transactions with related parties.

As with the other antideferral regimes, the CFC rules can cause a cash-flow problem for shareholders who are taxed on income that is not distributed to them by the corporation.

Again, investments in a CFC require a number of forms that must be reported when investing, and on an ongoing basis. Thus, it is often advisable to avoid accessing international investments using a foreign corporation so that you are not subject to the CFC rules.

As you can see, while the investment opportunities are endless, the ways in which you can access them can be tricky to navigate. So how can you diversify into safer and potentially more lucrative investments if you can't even get access to them or if it's prohibitive to do so? You will need some way to access all of these compelling investments and at the same time be completely compliant without suffering any negative tax consequences or other penalties. The twenty-first-century saver and investor should not be deterred. There are ways to overcome all of these obstacles, and these will be discussed later in the book.

STEP 2: PROTECT YOURSELF FROM THE ERODING U.S. DOLLAR

In terms of protecting and growing buying power over the long haul, twenty-first-century savers and investors must diversify outside of their home currency. But before you flip the page because you don't consider yourself a "currency trader," you should know that the currency markets provide opportunities for every investor. Here, we'll be focusing primarily on long-term ideas. We'll leave the trading platforms, Fibonacci charts, and day trading to someone else.

If you look at history, there have been countless currencies that have depreciated to the point where they become obsolete. Like dead languages, populations eventually cast these currencies aside and replaced them with stronger, better-managed currencies. Most recently, the euro replaced over a dozen currencies including the French franc, German deutsche mark, and Italian lira.

If you're looking for an example a bit closer to home, look no further than the U.S. dollar. The U.S. dollar (much like the United States) used to be the strongest, most respected currency on earth, tied to the world's largest economy.

But now the dollar tells an entirely different story. Your so-called trusty U.S. dollar has been pushed downhill over the last century.

Currencies, like the U.S. dollar, are an investment in a country's government—a bet that they'll be able to protect and grow real wealth in the long term. In "buying" a currency, you're actually investing in a country's strength, economic policy, political stability, and dozens of other factors. Whether you know it or not, chances are you are already heavily invested in the currency markets, specifically the U.S. dollar. If you have a U.S. bank account, a stock portfolio, an IRA, or a 401(k), you are a currency investor.

You can think of currency investing like buying or owning stock in another country. Just like you wouldn't buy a company just before it files for bankruptcy, you shouldn't buy or own a currency connected to a country drowning in debt. You want to buy and own currencies that will hedge against the downfall of your home currency.

But if you're concerned with the long-term effects of your native currency—and if you are an American, you should be—there is no need to worry. Assuming the worst should happen and your currency drops in value, there will always be another currency rising against it, thus a way for you to profit. In the following pages, we'll reveal how the dollar got to where it is today, why we don't have much hope for it in the future, and how to hedge against a future where the value of the U.S. dollar is unknown.

Dollar Holders Locked Inside a Sinking Ship

As the citizens of Russia and Argentina have learned—and Americans soon will—the government isn't an entity you can trust to protect your wealth. As you can plainly see in Figure 2.7, the dollar has been sinking in value over the last quarter century.

Since the creation of the Federal Reserve in 1913, the value of our currency has collapsed. What was worth $1 back then is worth only 4.8 cents today! That's a 95 percent devaluation of your money. And there really is no bottom. Just think about it for a minute. If you take $1,000 and devalue it by 90 percent, you have $100. Devalue that by 90 percent and you're left with $10. Take away another 90 percent and you have $1. Another 90 percent and you're down to a dime. Then a penny. Then fractions of a cent.

And the news hasn't gotten any better in recent years. Just during your lifetime, the dollar has declined heavily. From 1976 to 2009, the U.S. dollar lost an average of 73 percent of its purchasing power against most major currencies! That means $100,000 would only be

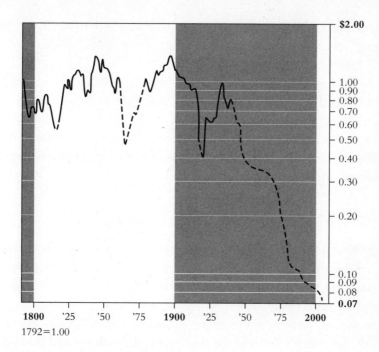

1792=1.00

Figure 2.7   Greenback's Purchasing Power

Source: Chart by American Institute for Economic Research, from the Wholesale Price Index complied by the Bureau of Labor Statistics.

worth $27,000 today. Yet, if you had just held your "cash" portfolio in Swiss francs or Japanese yen during that time, your portfolio would be worth $157,000 to $187,000 today.

Even worse, in the past seven years alone, you've gotten even poorer—a lot poorer.

Since 2000, your most basic costs of living have soared. Your grocery bill is up 19.9 percent. Medical costs have bloated by 34.6 percent. Your utilities at home have soared 45.5 percent!

Investments over the same seven years *lost* 1.2 percent annually. A $500,000 portfolio shrank to $459,482. And a $60,000 salary in 2000 has dwindled to $47,755 under inflation's crushing pressures.

You're paying more for everything, yet earning less at the same time. And predictions for the dollar's future are even more grim.

Average investors think the government or the Fed has some magic bullet that can reverse this trend. They're wrong. They can't stop this dollar devaluation because they created it. And now their "print-ing press" response to the most recent credit crisis will only seal the dollar's fate.

How is this possible? One word: *inflation*. What you could have bought for only $1 in 1980 now costs you $20, and in another 5 or 10 years, it'll cost you even more.

This is the ugly reality of the Federal Reserve. To understand how we got here and why the dollar will continue its downward trend, let's take a look at the basic concept of money.

The Birth of a Worldwide Fiat Money System

Money is nothing more than a medium for exchanging goods and ser-vices. In the early days of civilization, bartering was an accepted form of transacting business where people could exchange goods for other goods of relative value.

Under this system, there were no standardized prices per se, but rather things were valued based on the need for them and their supply. And, in general, it worked relatively well.

But the barter system had some practical limitations.

First, when bartering, dividing payment was often difficult if not impossible altogether. If you took a cow to market and traded it for 10 bushels of grain from the local elevator, that was fine. But if you took a cow to market and wanted to buy two bushels of grain, a few bolts of cloth, and some tools, you had a problem. There was effectively no way to "make change" for your cow.

It also created a problem on the business side, especially where accounting was concerned. It became virtually impossible to figure one period's profits against another. If you earned two cows in one month versus a hog, four wagon wheels, and 100 yards of rope in another, how were you doing? Were you worth more or less?

These limitations posed serious problems where the issues of exchange were concerned and eventually gave way to the need to standardize money.

Originally, a medium of exchange—a currency—was thought to require its own inherent value. Something of value on its own. For centuries, even millennia, precious metals were the commodity used in this capacity. They were ideal for the purpose.

First, they were considered valuable on their own. But at the same time they weren't so rare that there was limited access. Second, they were portable and easily divisible, which meant you could carry an amount around with you wherever you went. And you could buy whatever you needed in the quantities you desired. Finally, they were homogeneous and durable. They could be minted into identical coins and would last a long time—all the ideal traits for a form of currency.

And gold, as a commodity, was deemed perfectly suited to this task.

The Brave New World—Creating Money without Value

Everything in the world has inherent value—a value in and of itself based on what it provides you. Your car gets you to and from work. The food you buy at the store feeds your family. Tools you may have in your garage help you fix things up around the house.

And the value of everything is determined by its supply relative to the demand for it—except, that is, for money today. The Federal Reserve has seen to that.

The gold system worked well for decades, until the U.S. government had to pay for an ever-growing public debt from entitlements and to finance a war. By the late 1960s, politicians discovered they simply did not have enough tangible gold to back the dollars needed to pay off those debts.

So President Richard Nixon decided to change the system. In August 1971, he officially abandoned the link between the U.S. dollar and gold.

Today, the value of money is based solely on what someone will give you in exchange for it. Period. And it could be produced virtually at will. That is, in fact, the great irony—the very currency we use as a medium of exchange has absolutely no intrinsic value (see Figure 2.8).

How much is a dollar worth? Today, it's worth about a pack of gum. Maybe a 12-ounce can of soda? A few years back, however, it might have bought you two packs of gum. People will say the price of gum has gone up, which is true. But what has also happened is the value of your dollar (in terms of gum or soda) has gone down. Why is that?

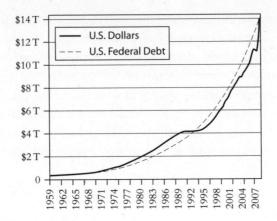

Figure 2.8   U.S. Money Supply

Source: www.Chrismartenson.com.

Money can't be consumed or used up like any other physical commodity. Money is only a medium of exchange. All it does is facilitate the transfer of goods and services. If the supply of a commodity rises above the amount that a society will consume for whatever reasons, its price comes down until demand picks back up.

Money, however, is a tool of demand. The greater the supply of money in circulation, generally, the greater potential demand for everything else. This then drives real asset prices higher and higher, thus in effect devaluing its own purchasing power.

Interesting twist, isn't it?

What Drives Currencies

As we mentioned, currency prices around the world are set purely on individuals' supply and demand for that currency around the world. This supply-and-demand system stems from the need to facilitate global trade of goods, services, and capital. However, there are other drivers behind the world's major currencies that create this effect. And while currencies move and change prices based on a whole host of obscure relationships that are best left to the professionals to analyze, there are several factors that contribute to the demand of currencies around the world. Understanding these factors will help lay the groundwork to help you diversify outside of the dollar.

- *Interest rates.* Interest rates are the ultimate "inflation gauge," and inflation directly affects a currency's value. All currencies have an associated interest rate, which, at least in the short term, is largely determined by that country's central bank. Interest rates are strongly linked to currency values. Changes in interest rates can have an immediate impact on the strength or weakness of a currency. Interest rate hikes typically have a positive impact. They attract foreign investors, who bid up the value of the currency. Then, as the currency gains strength, it can attract even more investors seeking the opportunity to make a profit.
- *Economic growth.* When a country's economy is among the strongest in the world, it tends to attract more investment capital, helping to drive up the value of its currency. Conversely, when it's among the weakest, it attracts less investment capital or may even suffer a net outflow of capital as international investors seek greener pastures.

  Plus, economic growth means there is more money floating around in the system, so when this happens, central banks usually take action in order to contain all this loose money. Normally, it will take money out of the system by hiking interest rates, which, as we just discussed, is very good news for the country's currency.
- *Trade deficits.* Typically, a large trade deficit is very negative for a currency's value. For example, the U.S. trade deficit rose to its highest level ever in 2008. Exports were at an all-time low, while imports were at an all-time high. This created an ugly imbalance for the U.S. economy.

  In order to buy goods abroad, the U.S. had to sell its own currency, and the more you sell your own currency in exchange for foreign currencies, the more your money will fall in value. In addition, with more money exiting the country than being brought in, the currency will suffer even further devaluation.
- *Inflation.* Higher interest rates are not a direct magnet for international money; instead, they run through a filter—inflation. The rate of inflation is actually the common factor that all central banks around the world use to determine what they'll do with interest rates. When inflation rates are down, banks tend to cut interest rates to stimulate the economy. However, during high inflation, banks will increase the interest rates to discourage

lending and spending. Hiking up the interest rates boosts the value of the currency.

- *Political stability.* For the most part, the true drivers of a currency are the sustainable, long-term economic forces. The one exception would be a country that suffers from sustained, chronic political instability.
- *Market psychology.* This is one of the most interesting driving forces because sentiment isn't governed by any concrete data or facts. Instead, sentiment is driven by the people who trade the market. It's the market "mind-set"—the collective views of all the traders in the forex market. In many cases, expectations alone can drive a market up or down.

So what does all of this mean to the twenty-first-century saver and investor?

Armed with this information, you can begin seeking out ways to structure your portfolio using currencies that will hedge against the volatility in the U.S. dollar we are seeing now and will continue to see well into the future.

The currency markets provide you with the potential for greater returns no matter what your investment horizon. Whether you are a short-term trader or you are building a diversified portfolio for the long term, currencies can boost your total return.

An Eternal Bull Market

First and foremost, currencies are the only asset with an eternal bull market. The value of a currency is based on how it measures up to other currencies. You see, you can only judge how much a foreign currency is worth based on how it measures up to your own currency. For example, if you went to Switzerland, you would only know what you were paying if you converted the Swiss franc into U.S. dollars. Otherwise, the exchange is meaningless.

When you're looking at two different currencies, one currency is always worth more than the other. And as one currency rises, another one falls at the same time. The currency rates are constantly changing, and when one goes up, one must come down, kind of like a seesaw.

Furthermore, regardless of any external factors, one will always rise in relation to the other, thus creating the eternal bull market.

Hedge against Market Risk

In contrast to stocks, bonds, and commodities, it is impossible for all currencies to crash at the same time. Individual currencies can certainly fall and surge against others. The depreciation of one currency is automatically linked to the appreciation of another; therefore, a crash affecting the entire market is simply not possible.

Greater Profits from Traditional Investments

Global market investments provide an unprecedented opportunity to profit from a new generation of emerging markets. Currencies are merely an extension of that.

Denominate those investments in a foreign currency and not only will you be dealing with greater margins of profit, you'll be hedging against the uncertainty of the dollar.

Anytime you can purchase an offshore investment that's denominated in a foreign currency like the euro or the Japanese yen, you have the potential to earn additional profits if that currency rises against the U.S. dollar. For example, say you bought shares of Switzerland's largest bank, and your investment rose 13 percent over nine months in Swiss francs. Now suppose that the Swiss franc rose 4 percent against the U.S. dollar over that same period. That means you pocketed an additional gain of 4 percent, for a grand total of 17 percent, just because you bought an offshore stock denominated in a different currency.

Dollar Holders Are Way Behind the Currency Times

The United States is way behind in the currency trading business. The average U.S. investor has no idea how to even access the currency market. Granted, one of the reasons for this lack of know-how is where the United States is located. Over the centuries, Europeans have become accustomed to changing money at borders even on long road trips, while most Americans have to jump on a plane to get the same experience.

Also, we can thank U.S. banks for this ignorance. Most U.S. banks simply don't offer these types of products. In fact, the only U.S. bank that we know of that is able to offer foreign currencies, including deposit accounts and certificate of deposit, is EverBank (Appendix B-3).

But today, it's easier and more important than ever to take full advantage of all the protection and profitability that currencies offer.

Currency diversification could range from a simple investment in a foreign stock market, foreign bonds, or anywhere the currency of choice isn't U.S. dollars. You can even simply hold your cash in Australian or kiwi dollars instead of the American dollar. In one fell swoop, you'd be tapping into a promising foreign market and shifting a bit of your wealth away from the U.S. dollar.

But this isn't some kind of "insider tip" on how the professionals get ahead; currency diversification is merely a fact of life in most countries around the world. Savvy citizens in Argentina hold U.S. dollars by banking in Miami, wealthy Russians diversify across oil-rich Middle Eastern companies, and Indian citizens have an undying fascination with all things gold.

Currency Investments for the Twenty-First Century Portfolio[1]

Though it takes time and lots of real world experience to take advantage of the most profitable opportunities available to you in the currency markets, the following list is a good resource to help identify key currencies that, at the very least, might help to hedge against a further falling dollar.

Australian Dollar (AUD or A$)
Central Bank: Reserve Bank of Australia (RBA)[2]

With an economy based strongly on commodities, Australia tends to prosper during commodity bull markets. Australia is the third-largest producer of gold and is rich in energy resources. As a commodity-based currency, the Australian dollar is a popular currency with investors during inflationary environments when there's a growing need for raw materials. Another factor that investors appreciate about Australia is the government's policy to discourage intervention in the foreign-exchange market.

- Australia's key industries include mining, industrial and transportation equipment, food processing, chemicals, and steel.
- The Australian dollar generally tracks the price of gold because Australia is such an integral gold producer.

Brazilian Real (R$ or BRL)
Central Bank: Central Bank of Brazil[3]

After their currency depreciated sharply in 2001 and 2002, the Brazilian government implemented an aggressive economic program to curb inflation and reduce debt.

Afterwards, Brazil enjoyed increasing economic growth and increases in employment and real wages for the major part of the 2000s. While this growth has had a positive impact on Brazil's economy, a quarter of the population remains below the poverty line. As the largest economy in South America and a growing presence in the world markets, Brazil gained the confidence of many foreign investors—at least prior to the credit crunch of 2008.

- Brazil has the second-largest oil reserve in South America, and the country became a net oil exporter in 2007.
- As an emerging market, Brazil's economy and the value of the real can be susceptible to the fluctuation of global risk aversion.

British Pound (GBP or £)
Central Bank: Bank of England (BoE)[4]

Informally known as the pound or quid, the pound sterling has been a popular choice among investors for longevity and strength. The United Kingdom's economy has historically been one of the strongest in Europe, even though the credit crunch put a damper on their long-term growth in 2008. Still, the pound enjoys its status as one of the most traded currencies in the foreign exchange market. In fact, the pound is also known as the "cable" because the GBP/USD pair was once traded via transatlantic cable.

While Great Britain is a member of the European Union (EU), the country's government has chosen not to adopt the euro and debates the level of economic interaction it should have with the EU. The outcome of this debate could have an impact on the country's trade freedom.

Canadian Dollar (CAD or C$)
Central Bank: Bank of Canada (BOC)[5]

The 13th-largest economy in the world, Canada enjoys strong economic ties to the United States. Foreign investors appreciate Canada's commodity-driven economy led by its oil reserves, during commodity bull markets.

Currently, Canada had the second-highest oil reserve in the world after Saudi Arabia. The value of the Canadian dollar, or loonie, is tightly integrated with fluctuations in commodity prices and the economic health of its largest trading partner to the South, the United States.

- As a commodity-driven economy, Canada benefits from rising energy prices. And demand from emerging markets could have a significant impact on Canada's economy.
- Canada is also the top producer of uranium.
- Slowdowns in global growth can affect Canada's export-driven economy. With 80 percent of Canada's exports going to the United States, slowdowns in the U.S. economy can have a dramatic effect on the loonie's value.

Chinese Renminbi (RMB) or Yuan (CNY)
Central Bank: People's Bank of China (PBC or PBOC)[6]

Currently pegged to the U.S. dollar, the yuan is considered one of the most undervalued currencies today. With a growing importance in the world financial arena, the Chinese RMB attracts attention from many leading investors. While considered primarily an exporting nation, a growing middle class helps China move toward a robust consumer economy. A strong element of China's economic growth comes from foreign investments.

- China is the world's largest exporter, with an account surplus of just over $135 billion.
- For over 30 years, China's growth rate has been the fastest of any large country in history.
- As an emerging market, China's economy and the value of the renminbi can be susceptible to political risks and fluctuation of global-risk aversion.

Czech Koruna (CZK or Kč)
Central Bank: Czech National Bank[7]

Centrally located in the European Union, the Czech Republic is considered by many to be one of the most stable and prosperous post-Communist states. The country, like the whole central and eastern Europe region, took a big hit during 2008's crisis. With a relatively low loan-to-deposit ratio, its banking system is one of the strongest of the region. Additionally, there is much anticipation of the koruna merging into the euro.

- As an emerging market, the Czech Republic economy and the value of the koruna can be susceptible to the fluctuation of global-risk aversion.
- The Czech Republic has postponed the adoption of the euro from the planned year of 2010 to no sooner than 2019. Future adoption is uncertain due to European Union rules. Once the Czechs commit to a date, the country must meet economic thresholds and undergo a minimum two-year test of currency stability.

Danish krone (DKK or Kr)
Central Bank: National Bank of Denmark[8]

The krone (kroner, plural) is known to many as a stable currency, representing a stable Danish economy. The economy definitely meets the EU's criteria to adopt the euro. Although Denmark opts to keep the krone, its value remains pegged to the euro.

- Its industrialized market economy depends heavily on the service sector.
- The economy is stable. Inflation and unemployment remain low.

Euro (EUR or €)
Central Bank: European Central Bank (ECB)[9]

The Eurozone includes members of the European Union that use the euro as their common currency. Considered a major global reserve currency, second to the U.S. dollar, the euro was formally put into circulation in 2002, but official trading for the currency began in 1999. The euro is a stable currency from one of the world's largest trading powers, so it has become an alternative currency to investing in the world's reserve currency, the dollar.

The 16 European Union member states, known collectively as the Eurozone, are: Austria, Belgium, Cyprus, Finland, France, Germany, Greece, Ireland, Italy, Luxembourg, Malta, the Netherlands, Portugal, Slovakia, Slovenia, and Spain.

- The euro was first introduced at $1.18 (EUR/USD) in 1999.
- Currently, the euro is considered the "King of Currencies" among currency traders. That's why the euro is always listed first in every currency pair—even before the British pound.

Hong Kong Dollar (HKD or HK$)
Central Bank: Hong Kong Monetary Authority[10]

In 1997, Hong Kong became a special administrative region of China with a high degree of autonomy to manage its monetary system. The country has ambitions of being the primary international financial center for Asia. The Hong Kong dollar operates under a monetary policy that strives to maintain currency stability. To accomplish this, the Hong Kong dollar can trade within a range of $7.75 to $7.85 to the U.S. dollar.

- As Hong Kong's top source of investment and tourism revenue, China's growing economy benefits the country by potentially shielding it from any weakness in the U.S. economy.
- Hong Kong is competing with Shanghai, Tokyo, and Singapore to become the international financial center in Asia.

Hungarian Forint (HUF or Ft)
Central Bank: Hungarian National Bank[11]

Since becoming a democracy in 1989, Hungary has transitioned from a centrally planned economy to a market economy. Hungary has struggled with high inflation, which challenges its export-oriented state. In 2004, Hungary joined the European Union (EU) and started the process of converting the forint to the euro. However, the recent global recession will probably delay this process.

- In the long term, the Hungarian forint could strengthen as the country transitions toward the adoption of the euro. Experts do not expect adoption of the European Union currency before 2014.
- As an emerging market, Hungary's economy and the value of the forint can be highly susceptible to fluctuations in the global marketplace.

Icelandic Krona (ISK or Ikr)
Central Bank: Central Bank of Iceland[12]

With a population of only 300,000, Iceland is one of the smallest economies to have its own currency. Iceland's economy depends heavily on exports, primarily from the fishing industry, which accounts for 70 percent of export earnings. Prior to the country's credit crunch–induced crash in 2008, the Icelandic krona was popular with currency investors attracted by the high interest rates the Central Bank sets to help control inflation.

- Iceland's high interest rates, used to help curb inflation, once made the krona a popular speculative currency for investors.
- As an emerging market, Iceland's economy and the value of the krona are *very* susceptible to the fluctuation of global risk aversion, which is a major reason why the krona crashed in 2008. Due to its small economy and inflationary issues, the Icelandic krona has always been very volatile in the global markets.

Indian Rupee (INR or Rs)
Central Bank: Reserve Bank of India (RBI)[13]

Poised to become a key participant in the global economy, India is the second-fastest-growing economy in the world. Many investors and corporations see enormous potential in India, from the retail side of a growing middle-class population to economic policies that promote financial globalization. Foreign direct investment has been a crucial factor for the record appreciation of the rupee in recent years.

- As an emerging market, India's economy and the value of the rupee can be susceptible to the fluctuation of global-risk aversion.
- As the rupee strengthens, concerns always grow over the impact of more expensive exports on the economy.
- Poor infrastructure throughout the country remains an obstacle for doing business in many parts of India.

Japanese Yen (JPY or ¥)
Central Bank: Bank of Japan (BoJ)[14]

Japan is the world's second-largest economy and is largely dependent on export growth. A population of over 127 million makes Japan one the world's largest markets. The BoJ has a tendency to set low interest rates for the country, so the yen has been a popular currency with investors during the past decade to use for carry trades.

- Japan imports all of its oil, so whenever oil prices rise, it causes stress on its export-dependent economy and impacts the value of the yen.
- Volatility in the global financial markets and, in turn, the carry trade, pressures appreciation of the yen, which can affect the competitiveness of Japanese exports.

Mexican Peso (MXN or Mex$)
Central Bank: Bank of Mexico[15]

The 12th-largest economy, Mexico has a free-market and export-oriented economy. For the last several years, they've experienced modest growth of about 3 percent per year. And since signing the North American Free Trade Agreement (NAFTA) in 1992, Mexico started shifting the economy from relying heavily on oil exports to exporting nearly 80 percent of Mexican-built products to the United States. Signing NAFTA led to a tight alignment of the American and Mexican economies, which has helped reduce the range of currency fluctuations between the peso and dollar.

- Since the economy is still highly dependent on oil exports, the currency tends to move in the same direction as oil prices.
- The financial crisis drove Mexico to the verge of fiscal crisis. But government has announced plans of labor, energy, antitrust, and political reforms to boost growth.

New Zealand Dollar (NZD NZ$ or Kiwi)
Central Bank: Reserve Bank of New Zealand[16]

Greatly dependent on international trade, New Zealand's economy benefits when Australia's economy benefits and vice versa. Considered one of the most business-friendly countries, they enjoy one of the lowest unemployment rates in the developed world. The New Zealand dollar, or kiwi, is a commodity linked currency and, due to relatively high interest rates, a popular currency to purchase for carry trades.

- As a commodity-linked currency, the kiwi tends to appreciate when commodity prices increase.
- Any slowdown for the global economy tends to curb this country's export demands, which can affect the kiwi's value.

Norwegian Krone (NOK or kr)
Central Bank: Bank of Norway[17]

A country rich in natural resources, Norway is the fourth-largest net exporter of oil. Its population enjoys one of the highest standards of living in the world and a generous pension program fueled by oil revenue. Historically, oil price movements tend to impact the appreciation and depreciation of the krone.

- The government controls more than 31 percent of publicly listed companies in the country.
- The appreciation and deprecation of the krone is susceptible to the fluctuations of oil and gas prices.

Polish Zloty (PLN or zl)
Central Bank: National Bank of Poland (NBP)[18]

Poland enjoys what could be one of the strongest economies in all of Eastern Europe. The Polish economy benefits from the privatization of small- and medium-sized state-owned companies, as well as a liberal policy on establishing new businesses. Poland's entry into the European Union in 2004 and the expected transition to the euro has made the Polish zloty a popular currency with investors.

- The anticipation of Poland's switch to the euro alone is expected to boost the zloty's value.
- Transition to the euro is not expected before 2015.
- As an emerging market, Poland's economy and the value of the zloty can be susceptible to the fluctuation of global-risk aversion.

Singapore Dollar (SGD or S$)
Central Bank: Monetary Authority of Singapore[19]

Singapore's reputation as one of the world's most business-friendly economies helps attract investments from over 7,000 multinational corporations. A heavily trade-reliant country, Singapore ranks within the top 10 competitive economies in the world and is considered one of the most competitive small economies. The country's strategic location on major sealanes has helped build Singapore's strong economic power. Speculating on Singapore dollar's exchange rate can be difficult as the free-floating currency's value is tied to a basket of undisclosed currencies from the country's largest trading partners.

- Thirteen free trade agreements with countries including the United States help Singapore maintain its competitive position as the manufacturing and research and development center in the region.
- The Singapore government is investing hundreds of millions of dollars to promote and develop its biotechnology industry. This effort has already attracted major investments in pharmaceuticals and medical technology.

South African Rand (ZAR or R)
Central Bank: South African Reserve Bank[20]

Rich in mineral resources, South Africa is the world's largest producer and exporter of gold and platinum. While enjoying the biggest, most developed economy on the continent, South Africa also deals with significantly outdated infrastructure and poverty issues. A popular commodity currency for speculators, the rand can be extremely volatile due to fluctuation in commodity prices, inflation and political issues.

- Global risk events can drive foreign investors to drop riskier currencies like the rand. This would have a significant impact on South Africa's economy since its account deficit is funded primarily by equity portfolio inflows.
- As a major exporter of gold, the currency tends to appreciate when gold prices increase.

Swedish Krona (SEK, Swedish Crown or kr)
Central Bank: Sveriges Riksbank[21]

Sweden enjoys a high standard of living through an economy heavily oriented toward foreign trade. Trade accounts for more than 50 percent of their gross domestic product (GDP). The financial model of public/private partnerships provides a unique economic mixture of high-tech capitalism and extensive welfare benefits. Sweden has been a member of the European Union since 1995, but still the country has chosen to keep the krona as its currency and not convert to the euro.

- They rely heavily on foreign trade, so the Swedish economy is highly dependent on the economic status of its trading partners. This can make the krona very volatile.

Swiss Franc (CHF, Fr, or SFr)
Central Bank: Swiss National Bank (SNB)[22]

One of the world's most stable economies, Switzerland enjoys a reputation for highly advanced financial services, long-term monetary security and strong bank confidentiality. Considered a safe haven for investors, Switzerland thrives on foreign investments, especially during times of global risk aversion. A popular currency for funding carry trades, the franc is considered one of the most inflation-resistant currencies in the world. Considered a safe asset during global instability, the Swiss franc tends to react more on external events than domestic economic conditions.

- Historically, the franc has close to an 80 percent positive correlation with gold. As the price of gold appreciates, the likelihood of the franc doing the same is strong.
- While not a member of the European Union, Switzerland could become more closely integrated with its European neighbors due to bilateral agreements.

U.S. Dollar (USD)
Central Bank: Federal Reserve[23]

Naturally, the U.S. dollar still holds a certain prestige for being the world's reserve currency. This means that every major commodity is priced in dollars everywhere in the world. It's also the largest holding of any other major currency among global central banks and institutions. It's estimated about two thirds of all the foreign exchange reserves in the world are denominated in U.S. dollars. A change in the value of the dollar has major repercussions on exchange reserves at central banks everywhere. And it's why when you think of the forex market, the dollar is the dominant rate to consider.

- The dollar tends to have a "safe haven" quality during recessions, meaning investors park their assets in dollars to ride out the volatile markets. This tends to push the dollar higher.
- Besides being the world's reserve currency, the U.S. dollar is also constantly dragged down by a massive deficit that just passed over $11 trillion.

Moving Your Wealth Out of One Basket

It's nearly impossible to get accurate data on how many Americans currently hold currencies other than the U.S. dollar. Considering that only 33 percent of Americans even have passports,[24] it's our guess that an even smaller percentage has taken steps to diversify their investments into currencies from other nations. But this is truly necessary for long-term wealth preservation in the new century.

STEP 3: LOWER YOUR WEALTH PROFILE AND PROTECT WHAT YOU HAVE

In order to build a sustainable investment and savings plan for the twenty-first century, not only must you diversify into global markets and currencies, you must also be diligent about keeping the money and assets you've accumulated thus far. This may seem horribly obvious, but there is more here than meets the eye.

We live in the age of bankruptcy, divorce, "slip-and-fall" lawsuits, bogus malpractice suits, identity theft, and all kinds of crime. It's becoming increasingly difficult to hold onto the money you've made.

Even if you're innocent, it doesn't mean that a lawsuit will end in your favor. In the United States—as in other countries—you never know who a judge will side with. And even if you *do* successfully defend yourself, the legal costs can border on the unbelievable.

Frivolous Lawsuits Abound with No End in Sight

The statistics are overwhelming. Nearly every American business and every U.S. individual will be sued at some point in their life. An even greater number will be threatened with lawsuits. Despite these dismal statistics, only a slim percentage of Americans bother with any property protection considerations at all. Statistics show that people who make $50,000 a year or more in annual income will be sued on average once every 18 months by somebody for something.[25] The legal system in the United States, encouraged by contingency fees, runaway juries and the availability of punitive damages, is often described as predatory. The simple fact is that this system is a constant threat to your wealth.

Even in your daily life, things can happen that put your personal wealth at risk. If you're a landlord, for example, and someone gets hurt on your property—or even if you get into a simple car accident—claims against you and your property can be substantial. You can be sued for physical or emotional damages. Armies of lawyers wait in the wings, snatching up cases and making a living off the assets of unsuspecting savers. That might sound dramatic or frightening, but at the time of this writing, according to the U.S. Department of State, there are nearly one million lawyers in the United States, a number that represents over 70 percent of all the lawyers in the world. There are approximately 150,000 stray lawyers in California alone.

And they're scraping up work any which way they can these days.

No longer competing with GM or AIG for advertising time, you'll see attorney commercials even during the national news these days. "Have you been injured due to the fault of someone else?" Also, websites like www.whocanisue.com are popping up left and right, and for years attorneys have trolled the public for class action suits that might bring in enough fees to pay for that new Mercedes in their driveway.

A new lawsuit is filed every 30 seconds on average and unfortunately, industry statistics tell us that 78 percent of lawsuit defendants never thought it would happen to them.

Here's one poignant example:[26] Sarah, who worked for a wealthy small business owner, was driving her employer's children to school. While talking on her cell phone, she ran a red light and crashed into another car. The accident killed a family of three. State law stipulated that in such cases, both the driver and the vehicle owner were liable. Both the business owner and his wife were named on the car's registration, as they were on all of their personal and professional assets. Due to the lack of protection planning, the accident ultimately put all of the business owner's assets in jeopardy.

You spend most of your working life building your business or professional practice. Could you survive the cost of a catastrophic loss?

Entrepreneurs and Professionals Are at the Biggest Risk

As a testament to the hidden risks of doing business in the United States, many small businesses and professionals carry extraordinary financial risks that insurance alone cannot protect against. The medical profession is a perfect example of this trend.

In today's litigious society, few physicians dare wield a scalpel or stethoscope without ensuring that the premiums on their medical malpractice insurance are paid up. The risk that a single lawsuit might cost them and their families everything they've ever earned is too great. Malpractice premiums are often barely affordable, and even then the insurance doesn't cover many claims.

Making matters worse, reinsurance companies have redefined the term *gross negligence*, meaning the insurance company may not pay even though you're insured. As a consequence of all these factors, you simply must acknowledge the fact that your personal assets are always at risk. Whether that risk ever really materializes or not . . .

Asset protection is just good business. Yet many physicians don't realize that there are other steps they can take to protect their personal assets from the claims that might surface in their professional lives. Similarly impacted are property developers, builders, and entrepreneurs/business owners—even lawyers themselves.

You could be the savviest businessperson on the face of the Earth, but if things take a turn beyond your control, your company may fail. In 2007, for example, 28,000 businesses filed for bankruptcy in the United States. Just one year later, in the face of softening consumer demand, that number had ballooned to over 43,000.[27] Behind every single case there are business owners and board members whose personal assets and savings are at risk.

Divorce Is a Major Threat to Nearly 50 Percent of Today's Families

Divorces can be painful, not only emotionally but also financially. Lawyers and judges normally make the entire situation even worse and more costly. In America, divorce is big business—a $28 billion a year industry,[28] with average costs of a contested divorce reaching $15,000—enough to buy a new car.

Fifty-seven percent of marriages in America end in divorce. If you have two or more children or grandchildren, there is a high likelihood that someone in your family could be touched by divorce. And unless you take legal steps to avoid it, a good portion of any inheritance you may have left to them will be lost in the divorce proceedings to their ex-spouse.

Identity Theft Is Also on the Rise

Imagine having creditors hounding you to pay debts you never incurred—foreclosing on your legitimate property or even hauling you into court. You can't buy a house, rent a car, or open a bank account, all because "the computer" shows that you're a deadbeat. You know it's not true, but convincing anyone else that the computer could possibly be wrong is almost impossible.

This nightmare is called "identity theft"—the fastest growing crime in America. According to the U.S. Secret Service, nearly 10 million new cases sprout up each year. A "typical" victim's financial losses can run $36,000.[29] And this doesn't include what victims may have to pay to creditors defrauded by imposters. It includes only legal expenses, lost wages, and lost time.

No State or Federal Protection

As is becoming a theme throughout this book, you simply can't rely on state or federal government protections. State and federal laws that seem to offer protection rarely do. U.S. statutes cannot always be relied upon. That's because at any point, a judge could rule against you and seize your assets, despite a law on the books that should have offered protection.

Legal battles between debtors and creditors are often played out in bankruptcy court, so it is natural, then, that much of precedence for asset protection law arises in the context of bankruptcy proceedings. Because of this, having an understanding of the basic bankruptcy principles is helpful to determine which property "should" remain outside of the reach of creditors, even though you may never be in such a situation.

When an individual files for personal bankruptcy, property owned by the individual generally becomes part of the individual's bankruptcy estate. However, certain property is either excluded from the bankruptcy estate altogether, or may be "exempt" under federal or state law. In either case, the property remains beyond the reach of creditors.

In today's society, the majority of most people's total net worth is made up of their primary residence and the assets they've accumulated in their retirement plan: IRA, 401(k), or pension plan. Thus, it's important to know what protection is given by federal and state bankruptcy rules, yet all too often these rules offer very little in the way of real protection.

Your Primary Residence

Nearly every state has what is known as "homestead exemption" laws to protect owners from losing their home to creditors. This protects you against judgments from the areas we discussed earlier: frivolous lawsuits, divorce, malpractice, identity theft, bankruptcy, and more. Most homestead statutes were enacted in the 1930s, so the limits are generally very low; $5,000 to $25,000 is typical. A few states, such as New Jersey, have no homestead exemption. Other states protect your home from creditor claims with no limit to total value.

Protection Limits Can Greatly Diminish Your Security

A few states offer unlimited protection: Arkansas, Florida, Iowa, Minnesota, Oklahoma, South Dakota, and Texas. In these areas, the homestead law completely exempts a multimillion-dollar mansion's total value from attachment by certain unsecured creditors. That may be one reason O. J. Simpson lived in Florida before he took up residence in a Nevada prison.

Most states, however, assign a limit to the amount of protection offered by their homestead laws. These limits vary widely. For instance, an individual homeowner in California may be eligible for only $50,000 in exemption protection, while the same home-owner in Massachusetts would receive $500,000 in protection.

For example, let's say that as a single individual, your home is valued at $550,000, and it carries a mortgage of $200,000 against it. Your equity in the home is $350,000 ($550,000 − $200,000). If you live in California, you may use the homestead law to protect $50,000 of that equity, leaving $300,000 unprotected, which is not exactly a lot of protection. However, if you live in Massachusetts, your state's homestead declaration exempts all $350,000 of your equity from unsecured creditor attachment.

It's important to note that the homestead laws do not automatically prevent a forced sale of your primary residence to satisfy a creditor claim. In the preceding examples, if you live in California, the sale of your home could be forced to satisfy such a claim, since the creditor could be paid from the sale's equity proceeds over and above the amount the homestead law exempts from attachment. If you live in Massachusetts, however, the homestead law would exempt up to $500,000 of a sale's equity proceeds from attachment; in this case, there would be no point in a creditor's forcing a sale of the property to satisfy a claim.

So it bears repeating: you simply can't rely on state or federal government protections. As you can see, state and federal laws that seem to offer protection for what is most likely your most expensive asset rarely do. It's up to each of us to protect what we have using the best tools.

Your Retirement Nest Egg

Traditionally, the treatment of retirement plans being susceptible to attachments by creditors has largely depended on the type of plan involved. Assets in employer-sponsored, tax-qualified retirement plans such as pension, profit sharing, and 401(k) plans have generally been protected from the reach of creditors since the decision of the U.S. Supreme Court in *Patterson v. Shumate* (1992).

However, individual retirement accounts (IRAs) are not. Therefore, the extent to which IRAs are protected generally has been a function of state law, which again varies from state to state. Although most states have statutes protecting IRAs to some degree, many of those statutes contain limitations, such as a fixed dollar amount or an amount determined to be necessary for the support of the individual debtor.

(The thought of the court's deciding how much money you need to live comfortably is truly worrisome.)

In 2005 the U.S. Supreme Court attempted to extend the level of protection available to IRAs under federal bankruptcy law in the case of *Rousey v. Jacoway*. Unfortunately, the Supreme Court decided that IRAs are the only type of plans protected under a particular provision in federal bankruptcy law. In order to take advantage of that provision, a debtor still has to demonstrate that the assets are "reasonably necessary for the support of the debtor and any dependents of the debtor." This "support standard" generally has been interpreted to mean "basic subsistence," as opposed to the standard of living to which the debtor has been accustomed. Ultimately, therefore, the *Rousey* case did little to protect the IRAs of wealthy individuals.

The timing of the *Rousey* decision was ironic since the Bankruptcy Abuse Prevention and Consumer Protection Act of 2005 (BAPCA) was signed into law by President Bush just a few weeks later, on April 20, 2005. The general purpose of BAPCA was to tighten the rules for personal bankruptcies (measures long sought by the banking and credit card industries), but the new law also made significant changes in the area of retirement plans. BAPCA is generally effective for bankruptcies filed on or after October 14, 2005.

Under BAPCA, all retirement funds exempt from taxation are now protected from the reach of creditors. Since IRAs are covered by section 408 of the tax code, there is finally uniform treatment of IRAs and qualified plans in bankruptcy, with one exception that we will point out below. Most importantly, the protection of IRAs under BAPCA applies without regard to the state in which the debtor resides, and without regard to the extent to which the IRA assets are necessary for the support of the debtor and his or her family.

The exception is that the amount that can be protected is limited to $1 million. However, this limit is applied without regard to any rollover contributions from qualified plans. Therefore, under BAPCA, an individual can roll assets from a qualified employer plan into an IRA with the comfort that 100 percent of the rollover amount (and investment earnings thereon) is protected, without regard to the state or states in which they reside currently or at any point in the future.

All of these factors add up to one simple fact: smart twenty-first-century savers and investors need to create a specific plan that allows them to protect their family assets. The real challenge here is creating the right solution that provides real, concrete protection. The most important thing is to plan early. As the old saying goes, it's too late to buy fire insurance when you smell the smoke.

So what solutions are available? There are several—in fact, far too many to cover adequately in this one book—but we'll focus on the two vehicles that are in primary use today.

For True Protection, Give Your Money Away

Many of the simplest asset protection strategies involve placing assets out of reach of potential, future creditors by giving them away.

Asset Protection Trusts

One of the best methods for asset protection is an asset protection trust (APT). A trust is a formal legal arrangement voluntarily created and funded by a person (the *grantor*) that directs another person (the *trustee*) to take legal title and control of the grantor's donated property, to be used and managed for the benefit of one or more other persons the grantor designates (the *beneficiaries*).

The beneficiary of a trust receives income or distributions of assets from the trust and has an enforceable equitable title to the benefits, but does not control trust assets or manage trust operation (see Figure 2.9).

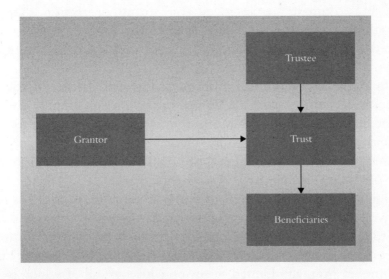

Figure 2.9 Asset Protection Trust Setup

Legitimate trusts can play a reliable and valuable role in the asset protection plans of high-net-worth individuals, especially medical professionals who could face losing their personal and family assets from catastrophic malpractice awards. Trusts can be formed either onshore in the United States or offshore.

Ten U.S. states—Alaska, Delaware, Missouri, New Hampshire, Oklahoma, Rhode Island, South Dakota, Tennessee, Utah, and Wyoming— as well as most offshore tax/asset financial centers authorize asset protection trusts that potentially can shield the assets of the person (also known as the grantor) who creates the trust from his or her creditors, at least to some degree. That's because assets donated to a valid trust are no longer the property of the donor, but belong to the trust.

In some states, property can be placed in a *spendthrift trust*—a restricted trust that pays income to a named beneficiary judged by the trust grantor to be too improvident or inexperienced to handle his/her own financial affairs. The trust beneficiary's creditors have no access to the trust assets, nor can the beneficiary assign or encumber his/her rights under the trust.

A spendthrift trust is a very strong and effective asset protection tool, but only if the beneficiary did not create the trust for his own benefit. If the beneficiary is also the grantor of the trust, the trust is referred to as a self-settled trust, and there is a good chance the spendthrift protection will not be honored.

A U.S. domestic trust gives you strong protection, but that strength multiplies many times over when the asset protection trust is located offshore in another country outside of the jurisdiction of U.S. courts.

Here's the reason why an offshore trust may be better for you.

If a U.S. court orders a U.S. trustee to do something, the U.S. trustee can be forced (by being thrown in jail for contempt) to comply with the wishes of the court. However, if a U.S. court orders an offshore trustee to do something, he could choose to simply ignore it. After all, he isn't bound by U.S. court decisions.

One of the most advantageous things about offshore trusts, as is the case with many offshore structures, is that an offshore jurisdiction doesn't have to recognize a U.S. judgment. This means that your creditor would have to start all over and begin the trial process from day one, bringing in witnesses from the United States or wherever, all of which is very expensive and time consuming. This is a huge deterrent to creditors and to contingency lawyers, who would much rather go after easy money and quick settlements. And even if the creditor brings the case to the offshore jurisdiction, he'll have to hire local representation and be certain that what he's claiming is "your fault" in the United States, and also is viewed as your fault under the law in the "offshore jurisdiction." In other words, the rules for "fault" are very different offshore than here in the United States. These nations aren't likely to grant judgment in your creditor's favor if he ordered a cup of hot coffee, spilled it on himself, and in turn sued you because it was hot and he burned himself.

In the United States, regardless of the state in which you form a trust, that state is required by the "full faith and credit" clause of the U.S. Constitution to recognize the judgment of any other state. This means that a creditor only has to take a judgment from one state and register the judgment in another state without having to retry the case. This is a very simple process that is done every day by collection firms. If this happens, then *voila!* The creditor is back at your throat.

While APTs, and especially offshore APTs, offer a great deal of protection, they can be costly to create and complex to manage. Also, you must keep in mind that there will be ongoing annual legal fees incurred for the lifetime of the trust. Another common drawback with APTs is that many people are not comfortable giving away their assets. They want to retain control and have access to the money in case they need it. The protection granted by these trusts comes when you give up your right to any control! Not an easy task for most of us. But for individuals with several million dollars or more at stake, a trust can be a vital part of a broadly configured asset protection strategy.

It is always important to confirm the U.S. tax consequences before creating any type of structure, and this is especially true when setting up a foreign trust, particularly if it is an irrevocable trust where you give up control, as this may trigger U.S. gift tax. This takes careful planning, and you must work with a U.S. tax attorney. Also, when working with international providers, it is important to stress that, as an American, you should always work in conjunction with a U.S. tax adviser or make sure they have obtained a valid U.S. tax opinion on their solution. Never assume that a foreign adviser understands U.S. laws. While the structure may not be liable to tax in their country, it very well may be in yours. Unfortunately, we have seen many trusts that have been set up incorrectly due to lack of proper planning, and it is very costly.

Family Limited Partnerships

The family limited partnership (FLP) is a separate legal entity, with its own unique tax identification number. Any FLP income or loss flows through to the partners, for which they are personally responsible in their 1040 income tax returns. Typically, family savings, investments, and titles to business and real estate interests are transferred into the FLP, which, if properly structured, protects these assets from potential claims and lawsuits.

Even if a plaintiff were to win a judgment against a partner, he or she would be unable to reach the assets held in the partnership.

In a typical FLP, you and your spouse or other family member retain only a small minority ownership in the partnership (1 or 2 percent), but also function as the general partner. As the general partner, you retain operating control of the partnership and its assets. Meanwhile, your children or other heirs who are partners own the bulk of the partnership in the form of limited partnership units.

The FLP works well for asset protection because the law in every state does not permit a creditor to seize or collect against property held in the name of the partnership. The property transferred to the FLP is generally safe from attack, but the creditor may attempt to reach your individual ownership interest in the partnership; however, that may add up to only 1 or 2 percent, thus safely shielding the remaining assets from attack.

These structures can be costly to create and complex to manage and remain compliant. The partnership will have to file its own tax returns, so yearly fees could add up. Also, we want to point out that the IRS in recent years has taken a dim view of FLPs, particularly with regard to the valuation of assets held in the partnership. This is a big issue because the valuation of the assets directly impacts the tax bill the partners must pay. It's important to work with a qualified professional and tax expert every step of the way.

Limited Liability Companies

The limited liability company (LLC) has become a widely used legal vehicle for accomplishing many asset protection goals. The LLC is one of the more versatile and convenient strategies for owning property and operating a business.

An LLC provides the protection from corporate liability without the cost of setting up a corporation and the formalities of corporate minutes, bylaws, directors, and shareholders. It's not uncommon for shareholders and officers of a corporation to be sued individually, forcing them to incur attorneys' fees to defend themselves. In contrast, LLC law specifically bars a lawsuit against an LLC "member" for the liabilities of the LLC. That is an important distinction that should be understood. A primary goal of LLC legislation is that members and managers of the LLC cannot be named in a lawsuit against the company. The main purpose of the LLC is to protect the owners from liability associated with the business.

The bad news, for physicians, lawyers, and some other professionals, is that state laws generally do not allow these professions to be operated as an LLC. The LLC liability shield available to business owners has not been extended to doctors due to opposition primarily from the trial lawyers. Although the LLC may be useful in protecting accumulated assets from lawsuits, it will not insulate the individual from the liability associated with a medical practice. As an alternative, many states have laws allowing professional associations (PAs) to be formed that offer some limited protection for professionals.

Timing Is Everything—Avoid Fraudulent Conveyance

It is important to recognize that asset protection planning is not something you do to avoid paying legitimate debts when you have the financial wherewithal to do so. Rather, it is a way to shield your personal assets from frivolous lawsuits, claims, or unreasonable jury awards related to medical malpractice or even personal liability claims such as automobile accidents.

Also, be acutely aware that you need to start asset protection planning long before any creditors are knocking at your door. If you wait until you've been sued, or even until you've done something that might trigger a pending suit, laws against "fraudulent conveyance" likely will quash any asset protection strategies you implement, on the theory that their main purpose was to deny creditors their claims.

With all this said, you certainly must understand that in order to keep what you have earned, you need some sort of asset protection in place as added insurance against the unforeseeable events in life. While there is no surefire way to shield all of your assets from future creditors, the strategies described here certainly can help.

STEP 4: CREATE A PLAN TO PROVIDE
FOR YOUR LOVED ONES

Discussing all the needs of the twenty-first-century saver inevitably brings us to a topic that might make you a bit uncomfortable—how to plan to care for your loved ones after you're gone. For many of us, this is *the* ultimate point behind our wealth creation and of our investment decisions.

Many philosophers and great thinkers have contemplated the inevitability of death and taxes. Benjamin Franklin is known for his famous saying that "in this world, nothing is certain but death and taxes." Despite his words of wisdom, there is often uncertainty when it comes to both death and taxes.

Unless we prepare for our deaths, there is uncertainty as to where our assets and liabilities will end up when we die. While no one likes to plan for death, the fact remains that no one lives forever. And procrastination can be your worst enemy.

Let's say you procrastinate until the relatively young age of 47. You're in perfect health, so you keep telling yourself "47 is the new 37. I have plenty of time."

Then tragedy hits. Whether it was a car accident or a sudden aneurysm, the result is the same. Your family is left without you, the head of the household.

On top of their grief, your family must also cope with the mess of the unplanned estate you left behind. If you're at all familiar with the "probate process"—the legal process that applies when a person dies with or without a will—then you know that probate can be a long and expensive. A lack of clear planning or a family dispute can lead to delaying the distribution of money and assets that may very much be needed by your family to sustain daily life. Your estate could be in limbo for years, possibly losing a majority of your wealth before it can be passed on to your loved ones.

Consulting an attorney for the drafting of your "last will and testament" is one of the strongest demonstrations for your loved ones that you really care about them.

Poor planning, combined with current estate tax levels, can make the whole experience into something resembling highway robbery as well. Assuming your business and other assets (or your "gross estate") are worth more than US$1 million, your family could be stuck with a considerable tax burden. At this writing, U.S. federal estate tax laws are in flux and very likely will be revised considerably by Congress during 2010. You can be sure that many families have to sell a large portion of their total estate just to pay income and estate taxes. Be sure to check with your accountant and/or attorney on the current state of the U.S. estate tax laws as each state varies. Knowing what your estate tax obligation will be at both the state and federal level will help do the proper planning.

Remember, the IRS considers your entire gross estate to include "cash and securities, real estate, insurance, trusts, annuities, business interests, and other assets." There are few exemptions that can be subtracted. For the most part, your estate includes nearly every asset you own, although the 2010 estate tax law revision is likely to exempt the first $3 million, if current plans being discussed become law.

As *Forbes* recently wrote, "You don't have to be fantastically rich to concern yourself with estate-planning issues." So the best way to plan for your estate is to simply prepare now, so you can move on with the rest of your life.

Getting Started on Your Estate Plan

The very first thing you must do is to take stock of everything you own. Your estate includes not only your personal belongings and investments but also your home, life insurance, retirement plan assets, as well as your share of any jointly owned property.

Next, consider how to divvy up your assets and save taxes doing it.

You should consider giving gifts to your heirs, because that can be done tax free in some amounts. A series of planned, annual gifts to each heir over a period of years can effectively reduce the giver's federal estate taxes to zero. This is true even though each person is limited in 2010 to a maximum of $13,000 annually given to each person. Gifts over that amount are subject to the gift tax.

One attractive exemption is that you can bequeath an unlimited amount to your spouse without paying any estate taxes on that amount. Unfortunately, this is not a very effective planning tool, since it merely postpones the tax bite until your spouse dies. For a means to avoid estate taxes on either spouse, talk to a qualified attorney and ask him or her to explain the "unified credit exemption amount" that is available to spouses in estate planning with trusts.

Finally, while your stock investments will be included in your estate, your heirs will get a tax break when they sell the shares. They'll receive what's called a *stepped-up basis*. Basis is the original cost of an asset, later used to measure increased value for capital gains tax purposes at the time of sale or disposition by gift or otherwise.

For example, let's say you bought shares of Apple at $80, the stock rises to $150 by the time you die, and you leave the shares to your daughter. If the stock rises to $170 before she sells, she will owe capital gains tax on just $20 per share: the difference between $150 and $170.

The Importance of Having a Will

If you do nothing else after reading this book, we urge you to put your legal affairs in good order by creating a will or taking the time to review and update your current will. As we mention above, if you don't have a will before your death, state law will determine who gets your property. A judge may decide who will raise your children, and either or both may not be whom you would have chosen. Writing such an important document can be daunting, but it doesn't need to be. Yes, nearly half of all Americans die without a will.

Once you've taken "inventory" of your assets and decided how you wish distribute them to your heirs, creating a will is the next logical step. If you are under age 50 and don't expect to leave assets valuable enough to be subject to estate taxes, you can probably get by with only a basic will. But as you grow older and acquire more property, you should engage in more sophisticated estate planning; we discuss these details later.

A last will and testament is a written document in which a person directs the postmortem (after death) distribution of his or her property. In the United States, state law governs the specific requirements of what constitutes a valid will.

If you die without a will, the probate court steps in and distributes your property according to the laws of your state, which may or may not coincide with your wishes. If you have no apparent heirs and die without a will (*intestate*, as it is called), it's even possible the state will claim your estate. Remember, wills are not just for the rich; your will ensures that whatever your assets—a family Bible passed down from generation to generation, an engagement ring, or that picture that hung above your sofa—will go to family members or other beneficiaries you designate.

Probate is a legal term, which means to "prove" a will. During probate, the court determines that your signed will is a genuine document stating how you want your estate to be distributed. Depending on the state in which you reside, the probate process could take a few days or many months, and depending on the complexity of the will, it can be an expensive process. Thanks to due process and frequent delays in the court system, your family may not have access to funds from your estate for some time, and that can become a serious issue if those funds are needed for living expenses.

If you have a will, it is important to understand that all of your assets—whether they are in the United States or abroad—will be subject to probate courts in the United States. If you have a foreign bank account, for example, that account this is part of your overall estate, and it may take many months or even years for your heirs to get access to the offshore funds, unless everything is structured in a special way so that foreign funds can bypass the court.

If you have any doubt on how long the delays can be, let us share the story of Richard R., an investment adviser in his early 50s. Richard's parents resided in southern France for the latter part of their life. In 2005, Richard lost his mother to a long and difficult battle with cancer. Richard was the executor of her estate, and from the time his mother died in 2005, it took 18 months for the entire probate process to be finalized and assets to be distributed to the beneficiaries. However, among other U.S.-based assets, Richard's mother had a bank account in France, and Richard was the named beneficiary on the account, which was worth approximately €50,000. It took Richard almost two years until the bank in France would release the money and transfer it to his U.S. account.

A little preplanning can help streamline or avoid the probate process altogether. A qualified financial planner or estate attorney can help you determine what's appropriate for your specific situation, but a few ways that you can avoid probate altogether are listed next.

A Living Trust Skips the Probate Process

A *living trust* is just what that term implies: a trust created while the grantor is alive. Once an estate-planning secret of America's richest families, living trusts today are even hawked to the masses in television commercials by struggling lawyers looking for clients (beware such appeals). Living trusts come in two basic forms: *revocable* and *irrevocable*. The form you choose will have a significant impact on trust operation and asset protection. Therefore, you must understand the consequences of each choice before choosing one form over the other.

The greatest advantage of the living trust is that its assets completely avoid the lengthy, costly probate court procedures, and it can be used much like a will to direct assets to named beneficiaries. Financial privacy is maintained, although the total value of the estate and a list of assets may be made public.

With a living trust, when the grantor dies, it is the trust, not state laws or the courts, that directs the manner and means of final disposition of trust assets. There is no need for a probate court to intervene since the deceased grantor decided when the trust was created how his or her wealth would be eventually distributed.

When the grantor dies, the living trust declaration directs the trustee to distribute the assets according to the grantor's wishes. Beneficiaries can be heirs, relatives, friends, charities, or a named group such as your grandchildren. Or the trustee can be ordered to hold and invest assets, paying out income over a set period of time, say "until they reach the age of 21."

Avoiding probate, however, does not necessarily avoid federal and state death taxes, which are imposed on trust assets.

The actual operation of a living trust begins immediately when the grantor signs the trust declaration and transfers assets to the trust. Compare this to the delayed creation of a "testamentary trust" created in a will, which does not become operative until the grantor dies.

As a rule, living trusts avoid many problems caused by a testamentary trust that is created under a will. And, because the living trust escapes probate, the beneficiaries are spared hardships during a time of bereavement.

The assets of a living trust, as with any trust, can, in theory, encompass all kinds of property, including cash, insurance policies, a private home, autos, boats, shares of stock, or ownership of a corporation. That kind of multiple asset mix is to be discouraged, however.

The living trust may also be useful for individuals subject to estate taxes. A typical living trust has no effect on taxes. A more complex living trust can greatly reduce the federal estate tax bill for people who own a lot of valuable assets. For example, an *AB trust*, though it goes by many other names, including *credit shelter trust, exemption trust, marital life estate trust*, and *marital bypass trust*, can be designed for married couples with children. Each spouse leaves property, in trust, to the other for life, and then to the children. This type of trust can save up to hundreds of thousands of dollars in estate taxes—money that will be passed on to the couple's final inheritors.

Living trusts are easy to create and require little ongoing maintenance. They afford an extra measure of protection against loss of control, and ensure that your assets remain out of the public record even after your death. However, they do not provide protection against creditors or divorce.

Life Insurance—A Good Tool for Estate Planning

Many families find life insurance to be an important estate planning tool. Life insurance can help your family pay off your debts, your burial expenses, and legal expenses, as well as any federal estate taxes that are due, all of which could eliminate a forced sale of assets to generate needed cash.

Many people, however, are unaware that some life insurance proceeds are taxable. Life insurance proceeds are subject to federal estate taxes if the policyholder owns the policies or if the proceeds are payable to their estate. If your policy includes the right to change beneficiaries, to borrow cash value, to select dividend options, or to change premium payment schedules, chances are the policy will be subject to federal estate taxes.

If your objective is to avoid having the value of life insurance included in your gross estate for federal estate tax purposes, you must give up ownership of the policy. To make sure beneficiaries fully benefit, your life insurance policy(s) should be owned in someone else's name, perhaps a spouse or children. In doing this, you can ensure that life insurance proceeds will not be included in the gross estate for federal estate tax computation purposes.

If your total estate, including life insurance proceeds from policies owned by you, is less than the amount subject to federal estate taxes, the form of ownership of your life insurance policy may not be of concern to you. But if your estate is above the exempted amount, work with an attorney or other qualified professional to evaluate any tax consequences of owning any life insurance policies to ensure that your overall estate planning goals and objectives are accomplished.

Naming your beneficiaries in your life insurance policy(s) is a very important consideration. A life insurance policy is a legally binding contract that directs the distribution of proceeds to designated beneficiaries. Make sure the policy is consistent with your wishes. A will controls the disposition of life insurance proceeds *only* if your estate is designated as the beneficiary.

Estate planning is very complex and is subject to ever-changing laws. This book does not attempt to cover all aspects of estate planning. Be sure to seek professional advice from a qualified attorney. The money you spend now to plan your estate can mean more money for your beneficiaries in the end.

THE SOLUTION? WORK TWICE AS SMART, AND MAKE YOUR MONEY WORK TWICE AS HARD

As you'll find later in these pages, we're pursuing one solution that will overcome most of the challenges that a twenty-first-century saver and investor might encounter. As you've seen in previous chapters, this includes the ability to ensure that your wealth has access to global markets, can legally avoid and minimize excessive taxation, has ways to preserve existing and future assets, and has solid strategies to care for your family after you are gone.

As we said, it's a tall order.

If you were seeking just one or even a few of these critical advantages (that's all you would have needed to get ahead in previous generations), then it would be a relatively straightforward path.

But as you bring yourself up to speed—hopefully, sooner rather than later—you'll find that the world is already changing significantly and that you'll need to adapt your own personal strategy in order to stay ahead of the game. As the Red Queen told Alice in Lewis Carroll's *Through the Looking Glass*, "Here, you see, it takes all the running you can do, to keep in the same place."

CHAPTER 3

AN AGE-OLD SOLUTION TO INSURE YOUR PORTFOLIO

Meeting All the Requirements of the Real World

Diversifying into foreign currencies, accessing the world's fastest-moving markets, tax minimization, easy estate planning—as you've read in the pages before this, these are the kinds of things that are necessary for today's investor to stay ahead of the financial curve in the coming century.

Going abroad is the key, but this is not always so simple. Most international banks will no longer accept American clients, and if they do, most of the investments may be restricted; as an American, you cannot invest in most foreign mutual funds and hedge funds, or even worse—if you are not careful about the tax compliance issues, you can suffer horrible tax penalties up to 48 percent or more in some situations.

Trying to find the ideal solution to all of the current risks and the potential future problems, plus seeking the best-fitting vehicle to satisfy your personal needs in an increasingly uncertain and ever-changing investment landscape, can prove a bit challenging. However, we think we've discovered one: a foreign private placement policy.

At first glance it might seem to a little "out of the way," but often the most profitable and substantial solutions are found only by taking a contrarian view toward the options at hand. And many of us wouldn't want it any other way. The more "out of the way" a solution may be, the more it is not a prime target for eager regulators or aggressive lawyers. Plus, its unique benefits will give you access to all of the world's top markets, including those "first generation" countries that are now starting to emerge like never before. You'll gain some of the most solid legal asset protection in the world, a "compounding" edge, by allowing you to defer taxes on the investment growth; you can expect your financial affairs to be kept private, and best of all, it's perfectly legal and IRS tax compliant, when structured properly.

A private placement policy is a contract with an insurance company, but it's very different from the traditional type of insurance products you may be familiar with, to say the least. Today, the most interesting and robust policies are issued by foreign insurers. We will introduce the various policies in just a bit, but first we want to start by looking at one of most familiar types of private placement polices and one that was created in the United States.

MEET THE HUMBLE ANNUITY—THE MOST WELL-KNOWN PRIVATE PLACEMENT POLICY

We believe that the world of private placement policies is a little-known gem in the insurance industry. They hold the answers to many of the growing financial concerns of the twenty-first century.

In the busy and boring world of finance, the word *annuity* refers to any terminating stream of recurring payments. This cookie-cutter definition often misleads investors, and they accidentally overlook all the uses of this financial solution. While the term *annuity* encompasses many types of income arrangements, most often it's used to describe an arrangement where an insurance company agrees to make a series of payments to someone for the rest of their life in exchange for a single, fixed premium.

For example, you give an insurance company $500,000 at age 65. In turn, they agree to pay you an income of $3,500 per month for the rest of your life. When you die, the payments stop. That's a typical annuity.

Another common example is for an annuity to be purchased, but rather than funding it with one, single premium payment, there are a series of periodic payments until such time as the buyer of the annuity is ready to retire. For example, if you're 50 years old and make monthly payments of $3,000 a month for 15 years, the same insurance company might be willing to give you a lifetime income of $8,000 a month when you retire at age 65.

Annuities have a rich history stretching across countries and centuries. But since we're talking about your financial future as a saver and investor in twenty-first-century America, we'll start right at home. What you will discover is that American annuities are not the right solution for the needs and challenges we are facing. However, it's important to understand *why*. You see, the developments that have occurred with the U.S. annuity have become the model favored by financial centers elsewhere in the world.

THE EVOLUTION OF ANNUITIES IN THE UNITED STATES

Annuities have been in North America since before the current U.S. federal government even set up shop. In 1759, a company in Pennsylvania was formed to benefit Presbyterian ministers and their families. Ministers would contribute to the fund, in exchange for lifetime income payments.

It wasn't until over a century later, in 1912, that Americans could buy annuities outside of a group. The Pennsylvania Company for Insurance on Lives and Granting Annuities was the very first American company to offer annuities to the general public.

Growth was steady from that point on, but annuities really started to catch on in the late 1930s. Concerns about the overall health of the financial markets prompted many individuals to purchase products from insurance companies. In the midst of the Great Depression, insurance companies were seen as stable institutions that could fulfill the income payouts that annuities promised.

At this time, the entire country was experiencing a new emphasis on saving for a "rainy day." In the early days of the Great Depression, Franklin D. Roosevelt enacted comprehensive U.S. annuity legislation alongside the Social Security Act. As we mentioned in Chapter 1, and as Roosevelt knew full well, Social Security could only be a supplement—and not a central source—of retirement income for future generations.

Roosevelt's New Deal unveiled several programs that encouraged individuals to save for their own retirement as well. It was around this time, too, that group annuities for corporate pension plans really started to develop. Annuities, and the insurance companies that offered them, benefitted greatly from this newfound enthusiasm for saving for retirement.

So U.S. annuity laws were formed, giving individuals the incentive to save for their retirement in a tax-efficient manner. Thanks to the flexibility and simplicity of annuities, they have taken many forms over the years, each time adapting to meet the needs of a new generation.

At the time, fixed annuities were the product of choice. A fixed-return annuity (or fixed annuity) is one where the insurance company guarantees to make payments of a fixed amount for an agreed-upon term of years or for the lifetime of the person or persons named as income beneficiaries.

Implicit in any fixed annuity contract is an assumed rate of return that the insurance company will pay to the policyholder. The rate of return is based on the deposits made by the policy owner. In order to profit, the insurance company pays out a rate of interest that is less than it expects to earn by investing the funds it receives for the contract.

Fixed annuities had guarantees of principal and a stated investment return that was backed solely by insurance companies. And while the income, or gains earned within the annuity, was tax deferred until the annuity payments began, they earned relatively unexciting rates of return and they didn't offer much protection from inflation. But fixed annuities supplied government workers and teachers with a reliable source of retirement income.

THE BIRTH OF THE VARIABLE ANNUITY

You may be familiar with the company TIAA-CREF. The Teachers Insurance and Annuity Association (TIAA) was formed by Andrew Carnegie in 1918. Today, it remains one of the largest financial companies in America, helping those in the academic, medical, cultural, and research fields plan for and live in retirement. The TIAA started as a fully funded system of pensions for professors. Carnegie recognized that colleges needed to offer adequate pensions in order to attract talented teachers.

When World War II ended, government grants made it possible for many returning veterans to go to college. The number of college graduates tripled between 1944 and 1950. This unprecedented demand for a college education led to phenomenal growth, and it meant that TIAA—now with nearly 600 participating institutions— was facing new challenges. During the 1940s, inflation averaged more than 7 percent per year, hitting a record 18.2 percent in 1946. Also, there had been another dramatic development outside of the economic arena. Increased longevity was radically changing the actuarial projections that had long been used to determine lifetime annuity payments. In just 50 years, the average life expectancy in the United States had increased from 48 years to nearly 70.

TIAA's pensions were meant to last a lifetime, and with lives lasting longer and the dollar shrinking, new strategies were needed. TIAA responded with a pioneering economic study and financial innovation. Over a period of 18 months from 1950 to 1951, a TIAA task force analyzed historical data to determine how a combination of a traditional fixed annuity and a new "variable annuity" funded by periodic investments in common stocks would have fared during the 70 years from 1880 to 1950—a span that included two world wars, several financial panics, and a severe depression.

The task force concluded that investing retirement assets in fixed-income instruments alone was unwise because of the inflation risk. However, market risk made the sole use of equities unwise as well. But a mix of the two provided the best possible protection against fluctuations in stock prices and changes in the value of the U.S. dollar.

Inflation had generally occurred during times of rapid growth. By investing in the companies that were generating that growth, a stock-based fund would offset the loss of buying power experienced by the income from a fixed-rate account. When stocks declined, the fixed-rate account would provide stability. This strategy is still highly used today by many in the financial industries to moderate investor risk.

To implement these conclusions, TIAA created the College Retirement Equities Fund (CREF), the world's first variable annuity, which began operation on July 1, 1952. The variable annuity allowed interest-type earnings based on more speculative financial vehicles, such as stocks or other securities, in separate accounts. While variable annuities offered certain guarantees of principal and could provide greater opportunity for growth then their "fixed" cousins, they also posed greater levels of risk for purchasers. In short, variable annuities placed some of a purchaser's earnings at risk through the issuer's involvement in securities and other investments. The variable annuity thus acted much like an early version of the contemporary mutual fund.

Later that year, an editor at *Fortune* wrote to a colleague: "I think this is the biggest development in the insurance-investment business since the passage of the Social Security Act."[1]

DOMESTIC ANNUITIES EXPLODE ONTO THE AMERICAN MARKET

By 1960, the first variable annuity products were being offered to the general public, alongside the first "insurance separate subaccounts." These accounts are maintained by insurance companies, but they are separated from the insurer's balance sheet. This was a big development because it meant that even in the event that the insurance company failed, these accounts would remain untouched and the investor would be protected.

Over the years, through the gradual expansion of the IRS, new revenue rulings gave birth to the modern-day variable annuity. The Tax Equity and Fiscal Responsibility Act of 1982 (TEFRA) reaffirmed the tax privileges of all annuities, and the U.S. annuity industry boomed into the twentieth century, as you can see from Figure 3.1. If you consulted a tax planner or asset manager at any time in the last 20 years, they almost certainly mentioned that you consider the prospect of an annuity, fixed or variable.

Keep in mind that America's fascination with annuities began as an alternative to supplement teachers' retirement. So the minimums for such policies were quite low—usually around $10,000—and due to the small scale, the fees associated with the policies were relatively high.

Yet it did give peace of mind to many investors and savers. Instead of the frustration of managing your own investments—constantly

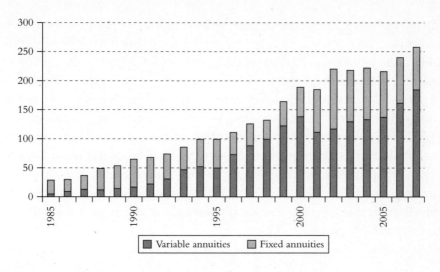

Figure 3.1 U.S. Fixed and Variable Annuity Sales 1985–2007
Source: Chart Courtesy of Swiss RE.

doing your homework and adjusting your portfolio—the annuity allowed you to simply sign a contract that guarantees, say, a 7 percent rate of return for as long as you're invested. No "ifs" and no "buts," no inflation concerns, and no tech bubbles or stock market bubbles to worry about. You could just expect a 7 percent gain each and every year, like clockwork. Kind of takes your money concerns right off the table, doesn't it?

But of course, nothing lasts forever. . . .

You see, these products exploded in popularity largely due to the current level of interest rates at that time. In order to minimize risk and maximize investment security, government debt was a primary investment vehicle for fixed annuities. And as you may recall, U.S. Treasury bond yields peaked around 14 percent in the early 1980s, slowly falling for decades to come. Falling interest rates meant you could buy a long-term bond that would not only beat inflation (which fell alongside interest rates) but give you a tidy, worry-free profit for your trouble.

If we fast-forward to today, we all know where interest rates stand—at about zero for most of the world's largest major economies. So these days, instead of 7 percent fixed return, you might be able to lock in a 1.5 percent return.

In that single connection, and with the stroke of a legislative pen to lower interest rates, the U.S. government pretty much took fixed annuities off the table for many American investors. Sure, they're still available, but in the current and foreseeable market environment they are not the investment that many investors want to own. Thus, by the raging bull market of the late 1990s, domestic variable annuities were exploding in popularity, while the interest in the fixed annuities had all but vanished.

While the variable and fixed annuities have been the most popular type of private placement policies in the United States, they are only one type of policy. In the past 20 years, there have been many new developments in the international insurance markets, and many investors are taking notice.

THE MECHANICS OF PRIVATE PLACEMENT POLICIES

Before going further, let's stop to consider the different persons involved in a private placement policy. Now remember, despite the flexibility and cutting-edge benefits of these solutions, they're still basically built around existing insurance laws.

Each policy involves at least three parties:

- The policyholder
- The insured
- The beneficiary

The *policyholder* is the individual who actually owns and controls the contract. Technically speaking, the policyholder can be a private person or a legal entity such as a company or special structure like a trust or a foundation. As you can probably imagine, in the event that a company or trust owns the policy, it's critical to consider the tax situation separately with a qualified adviser.

The *insured* is the person whose life the policy is linked to. When the insured dies, the policy comes to an end and the payout to the beneficiaries will take place. Due to the nature of this type of solution, however, the insured can be only a private individual. In some cases there can be two insureds, such as a husband and wife, and in this case the policy will remain in force until the last person dies.

The *beneficiary in case of survival* is the person entitled to receive payments from the policy as long as the policy is in force (e.g., annuity payments). Likewise, the beneficiary in case of death is the determined recipient of the policy's funds in the event of the insured person's death. The different beneficiaries can be private individuals such as a spouse and children, or maybe be a company or a legal structure such as a charity (see Figure 3.2).

In some cases, it's also possible to add an *arbiter* to the policy. This would be a third party who can be given certain rights defined in the "arbiter clauses." As you'll see in case studies later on in the book (Chapter 4 and Appendix A), an arbiter puts a name and a face on your plan. He or she is the person who can increase or decrease payouts, make adjustments to the plan, or preside over its liquidation. In short, the arbiter acts on your behalf to make sure your wishes are carried out. The arbiter is selected by the policyholder and can be a trusted adviser or a family member.

At its core, an annuity is simply a prearranged stream of payments from one party to another, much like a pension.

But as you'll see in the next few pages, this simple and straightforward vehicle has consistently risen to meet the demands of a changing

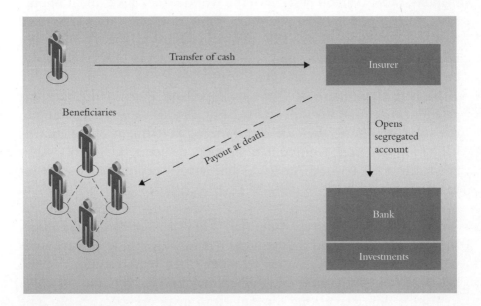

Figure 3.2 Structure of a Private Placement Policy
Source: NMG International Financial Services.

world. At times it's been mistaken for boring, but this staid alternative has always attracted a good deal of no-nonsense business because of its simple yet powerful ability to provide an income stream later in life or to provide for your loved ones.

SAVVY AMERICANS DEVELOP A LOVE FOR FOREIGN ANNUITIES

The annuity industry in the United States sprang up to meet the needs of John Everyman, with the first variable annuity being conceived for use by teachers.

While the United States offered some of the world's best investment opportunities and interest rates back then, as you read in Chapter 1, the economic growth and financial stability has been in a downward spiral ever since.

And American insurance companies failed to keep up with the times. Due to antiquated policies and restrictions, they have failed to modernize to meet the needs of today's investors. They fail to recognize that while the United States has the world's largest securities markets, more than 50 percent of the world's stock investment opportunities are found in other countries. Thus, investors with a U.S. fixed or variable annuity, have little to no exposure to the world's most promising opportunities. Plus, the only currency a U.S. annuity can be denominated in is U.S. dollars.

Sometime in the mid-1980s, and perhaps even before, a select group of American investors started to realize what was happening to the country: due to the lack of promising investment opportunities, falling interest rates, rising inflation, and a declining U.S. dollar, they needed to look beyond America's borders to secure their wealth for years to come.

Back in the 1980s and 1990s, the fixed annuity—especially the Swiss version—quickly became the "high flier" of the global insurance world. It attracted the world's financial elite, those creative souls with the time and the money to pursue rare opportunities and the keen eye to know a good thing when they find it.

And it didn't take long for American investors to catch on. The location of an insurance policy made no difference in terms of tax deferral in the eyes of the IRS, so savvy and in-the-know Americans started looking elsewhere to set up their fixed and variable annuity policies.

And it didn't take long before the U.S. government noticed this.

Remember, government debt was a primary investment vehicle for fixed annuities. And while the U.S. dollar continued to fall in value, along with Treasury yields and interest rates, over the decade, a strong Swiss franc and a 4 to 7 percent annual return of interest attracted many wealthy American investors. Money was leaving the United States for the safer, more profitable, and more conservative investment in Swiss fixed annuities.

In 1995, the IRS proposed new regulations relating to the federal income tax treatment of certain annuity contracts. The regulations determine which of these contracts are taxed as debt instruments for purposes of the original issue discount provisions of the Internal Revenue Code. The regulations provide needed guidance to owners and issuers of these contracts. As a consequence, foreign fixed annuities lost their tax deferral.

On February 9, 1998, the IRS changes came into force. Any foreign fixed annuity policies that had been created prior to April 7, 1995, were grandfathered in; however, from that point forward, foreign fixed annuity contracts were no longer tax deferred in the United States (Appendix B-4).

While one door closed, another door opened, and foreign variable annuities and other types of private placement policies came to the forefront of the market. Insurance companies around the globe are aware that tens of millions of people could benefit from what they have to offer, and they're ready to take some market share away from their less competitive and less hospitable competition.

WHY FOREIGN PRIVATE PLACEMENT POLICIES ARE THE BEST SOLUTION

Simply put, a policy can provide the open-ended structure necessary to meet the demands of a world where opportunity shifts around the globe. As we discussed earlier in the book, twenty-first-century investors and savers will find the best peace of mind in diligent diversification, not just in terms of currencies and cash holdings, but also in the field of long-term opportunities.

U.S. regulators are gradually closing doors and souring relations with foreign financial outfits, leading them to do the same. Due to the tradition and legal structure of private placement policies, however, their asset managers currently enjoy, and will likely continue to enjoy, one of the widest sets of investment opportunities available anywhere, period.

There's no special trick.

Many of the foreign policies, such as the offshore variable annuity, were originally designed as a carbon copy of U.S. variable annuities, in order to conform to the "letter of the law" for the IRS and the Treasury. So they enjoy the same tax deferral, but with the added bonus of superior currency and investment flexibility.

THE KEY TO A GOLD MINE OF INVESTMENT AND CURRENCY DIVERSIFICATION

Through your private placement policy, instead of a short list of long-only equity funds, you'll have the option to select an asset manager who can freely choose any investment he likes. He can cherry pick from the entire global investment universe without being constrained by your U.S. citizenship.

If you want a portfolio of emerging-market blue chips unavailable to most Americans, it's no problem. Want to create a portfolio that tracks the performance of a favorite fund manager like George Soros, John Paulson, or Bill Gross? You can make that happen. Your money will have the ability to be invested in literally anything from currencies, bonds, mutual funds, and commodities, to alternative investments like hedge funds and managed futures funds.

Let's stop and think about that. . . .

The latter two provide a whole new dimension to your tax-deferred savings, since hedge funds and managed futures funds will sell short and hedge in order to pursue *absolute return*, rather than solely buying and holding stocks to pursue *benchmark return*, as practiced at U.S. equity funds. All of a sudden, that single difference can give you a kind of all-weather performance you simply won't find in domestic insurance alternatives.

While pursuing a unique strategy determined by the policyholder, a foreign private placement policy can also help a U.S. investor to quickly and easily diversify out of currency risk.

Foreign currencies have already demolished the U.S. dollar as a store of wealth over the past several decades, and that's not likely to change soon. But shortly after your final annuity agreement is signed, a significant portion of your net worth can be transferred into euros, Swiss francs, Australian dollars or even silver and gold.

And don't underestimate the power of currencies as investments, either—at least as long as we're not talking about the dollar.

From 2002 to year-end 2008, the S&P 500 tanked by 10.8 percent, but the euro gained 60 percent, gold gained 201 percent, and even after crashing by 38 percent in 2008, the Aussie dollar returned 35.9 percent. To have had one of the best investment strategies on the planet, all you would have had to do was to exchange some U.S. dollars for an equal share of a foreign currency and gold coins.

While your first investment goal may be to own shares in India's up-and-coming blue-chip giants, you are also reducing your dollar exposure at the same time, giving you a little "dollar disaster insurance," while offering another dimension of profit. Native owners of the stock might enjoy a 30 percent rise in the value of the Indian company, but if the underlying currency strengthens against the U.S. dollar as well, then your position is looking even better.

Suppose you had established your policy in the fall of 2003, seven years ago. This was shortly after the introduction of the euro, and the international asset manager managing your account had a keen suspicion that the currency was destined for greatness in this decade.

Well, 2008 was a nasty year for stock markets across the world, but when you check your balance less than a year later, you find that your investments are still up 70 percent thanks to some strategic hedging, and despite sizable equity exposure. But then you remember to pencil in the open gain in currency terms as well, since the euro appreciated almost 25 percent against the dollar in that same period of time.

Of course, this is just a hypothetical case, and based on your risk tolerance, your investment adviser could create an investment plan even more unorthodox or exotic, but we hope you get the idea. We'll share some real-world examples in the case studies found in Appendix A so that you see what scenario best fits you.

ONE OF YOUR LAST OPPORTUNITIES FOR TAX-DEFERRED GROWTH

Investing through a private placement policy is simply one of the last bastions of tax-privileged growth available to U.S. citizens.

Remember again that U.S. citizens are taxed on *all global income and gains*. But when was the last time you paid capital gains tax on your car insurance?

That is to say that all insurance companies reinvest the premiums paid by clients. Combined with good actuarial work and prudent investing, an insurance company can make a tidy profit like that. Private placement policies function in a similar way, but technically speaking, you own your policy. The policy's value will be linked to the underlying investments. But since you don't own the underlying investments, taxes won't be triggered until payout, and your asset manager is free to manage your investments in a way that maximizes profit rather than simply minimizing taxes.

Plus, with properly structured policies, there are no passive foreign investment company (PFIC) or controlled foreign corporation (CFC) rules (see Appendix B-1 and B-2) that apply to you. And because of this, through your insurance policy, your assets can be invested in the lucrative global mutual funds we discussed earlier.

Depending on the type of policy, there are different tax benefits available (see Chapter 4) as long as the policy is created in a compliant manner. Most importantly, with most policies you don't need to pay taxes on the investment growth as long as you don't withdraw the money.

As you saw in the previous chapter, the ability to enjoy tax-deferred growth—reinvesting growth that would have otherwise been diverted into tax payments—can have an explosive effect on your bottom line.

100 PERCENT FLEXIBLE . . . 100 PERCENT OF THE TIME

One of the most important—yet most underrated—factors when setting up a specific investment solution is the ability to make adjustments.

Your life circumstances, legal and tax situations, and outlook on the markets—even your outlook on the political environment—will change over the years. So it's important for the benefit of your financial future that your money doesn't get locked into a rigid structure that is costly to maintain and even harder to change. With one type of foreign private placement policy, you won't just have an unparalleled degree of flexibility and access in terms of investing your money, but you can also liquidate, add to, withdraw from, and change your beneficiaries as your personal situation dictates.

Let's take a moment to explore what we mean by unparalleled flexibility.

Let's assume that you currently have $500,000 available that you can use to fund your policy today. But two years later, after an unexpectedly profitable piece of business, you find yourself with another $250,000 that you would like to add to your policy. It is not a problem because there aren't any limits on the amount of money you can add to the policies or the frequency with which you can do it. The same is true for withdrawals. Let's look at another example. You fund your policy in June, and just a month later you are faced with an unanticipated emergency. You'd be able to withdraw some of your funds from the policy without triggering a penalty or any additional taxes beyond what you would already face. (We cover the penalties and tax consequences in Chapter 4.)

With such flexibility, the foreign policy offers you 100 percent access, 100 percent of the time.

UNMATCHED INVESTOR PROTECTION

Now in this day and age, you might be skeptical about dealing with a foreign insurer. You're probably also wondering, "What if the insurer goes bust?"

It's easy to tell you to make sure you're investing only with top-quality institutions. But that alone won't do. Since the bankruptcy of Swiss Air—one of the highest-rated Swiss financial companies— you should always be prepared for the impossible in case it happens.

In such an event, your choice of jurisdiction often makes the biggest difference.

The right jurisdiction is the kind of place where the policy's underlying assets are fully segregated from the insurer's assets, in the event that the insurer fails. Remember, when you don't limit yourself to the United States, you can really pick from some of the finest financial institutions and protection laws in the world.

For example, Liechtenstein is a perfect home for your annuity policy due to the unmatched investor protection laws (Appendix B-5) where policy assets are always segregated from the assets of the company and the top-notch insurance companies that have chosen to set up shop in this country. There hasn't been one single failure in the 150-year history of the country's life insurance industry.

And there is good reason for that.

Choosing a home for your policy will be a major decision for anyone purchasing an offshore annuity, so we'll cover several jurisdictions, including Liechtenstein, in detail in Chapter 5. Needless to say, virtually every one of the available jurisdictions offers a greater degree of investor protection than you'll find with U.S. institutions—FDIC or no FDIC.

UNDER LOCK AND KEY

Another important consideration is the need for proper asset protection to ensure that your wealth is not ripe for the picking. Sadly, taking steps to protect your wealth is no longer an elective in the twenty-first century—it's mandatory.

Between the outrageous lawsuits, the expensive divorces, the million-dollar "slip-and-fall" damages, and all the other legal silliness that's come to dominate America's courtrooms, it should already be clear. If not, then the next few years will make it crystal clear, as hard economic times tend to bring out the worst (and most litigious side) in people. You've probably seen the evidence yourself—billboard advertisements for injury attorneys, television commercials inviting you to join in some obscure class action lawsuit, the proof is already out there—wealthy Americans *need* asset protection.

When you look to the world's top-ranked offshore financial centers (from Switzerland and Austria to Liechtenstein, Luxembourg, and the Isle of Man), you're talking about countries that have staked their reputation on the ability to protect and maintain those rights.

You see, the challenge for all developed countries is how to walk the thin line between having regulations in place that serve to *protect* the people and their interest without subsuming their whole sense of self-responsibility. In this book, you'll find some great examples of how these kinds of privacy and asset protection laws serve to *protect* citizens but don't provide places for criminals to hide.

But you're probably still asking, "Is this legal protection *really* better than the kind I find at home?"

Absolutely.

If you place your money with a financial institution abroad, this institution operates under the laws of the country where it is domiciled. So if there's a civil judgment against you in the United States and the judge orders one of your European-based assets to be seized, the European financial institution will not act on a U.S. court order. Your creditors will need to go abroad to the country where your assets are located, hire a local attorney, and try to seize the asset in that respective country. This all adds to the "psychological" edge of asset protection, since the implied costs in terms of time and money spent on hiring an attorney and engaging in the process are much higher, and in some cases forbidding.

We do want to be clear that the strong layer of asset protection we have discussed applies to civil matters and not to criminal ones. It should go without saying that if criminal matters come into play, there is virtually no protection available in any reputable country in the world. Asset protection is offered to honest citizens, not to scammers, thieves, or the like. Tough regulations are in place to prohibit any type of fraudulent or criminal acts in all of the top financial jurisdictions, and we applaud these measures.

By simply moving your assets outside the United States, you add a first layer of protection. Foreign laws, authorities, and courts must be involved. You're exposed to not only the U.S. system, but that of your chosen jurisdiction as well. But while setting up a plan to enjoy full legal asset protection can be more difficult, it ultimately provides significantly more peace of mind through a greater degree of protection.

Since the underlying investments are fully owned by the insurer, they cannot be seized by your creditors. If someone wants to attack your assets, he must go after your policy. If the policy was set up in the right jurisdiction and structured correctly, it simply cannot be seized or included in any bankruptcy estate. The policy will simply be seen as a nonseizable asset.

That simple fact paves the way for some of our favorite offshore anecdotes.

These anecdotes are almost always the exact same: an attorney chases down an ambulance after an accident or finds some knucklehead who burned himself on a cup of coffee or had a slip and fall while waiting in line at the buffet. The story begins like so many other lawsuits in America, with everyone breathing a weary sigh of concern, shaking their heads at the thought unfair financial compensation being awarded to the undeserving.

But then—what's that?

The attorney finds out that our defendant's assets are held in a carefully structured offshore insurance plan, spread out across the world, and in global jurisdictions known for their hostility to these types of nonsense lawsuits. Suddenly, the tables turn, and the attorney is the one shaking his head. He knows that to pursue those assets, he'd need to hire the services of an expensive foreign attorney . . . maybe even stake tens of thousands of dollars for a bond just to get his case heard.

The story then ends the way it should, with the plaintiff either getting nothing or only pennies on the dollar of his initial claim.

But the most important part here is that you plan early. With all solid asset protection plans, you need to make sure that nothing happens within a certain period, generally the first 12 months after the policy is set up. Otherwise, it must be assumed that you already knew about your situation when signing the application and that you tried to defraud your creditors. In that particular situation, you will not be protected.

If you are forced to declare bankruptcy or if there is a seizure of your policy within one year of establishing it or rather since the beneficiary designation was made, then it is possible to void your policy and your creditors may have a chance to access your funds.[2] The reason that most jurisdictions require a minimum term of 12 months is that if something happens within this period, it is assumed that you actually knew about your critical situation when you set up the policy, and thus it was your intention to establish an insurance policy to defraud your creditors.

After the 12 months, your creditors may still have a chance if they can prove your intent to defraud them—which now is possible only if you were insolvent at the time when you bought the policy—and that the beneficiary you chose knew about your intent. The creditor loses his right to request that your policy be voided after a period of five years, which is determined by the date that you selected a beneficiary for your policy. At this time, your money is fully protected.[3]

NO SECRECY BUT SUPERIOR PRIVACY

The days of utter secrecy, where you could have numbered bank accounts or use bearer bonds, are gone. And, honestly, we are not sad to see them go. The major world governments are working together to make sure criminals and other unsavory characters have nowhere to hide, and this makes global financial institutions much safer for everyone.

However, personal privacy is very important. The more you can take your wealth off the radar screen, so that a simple online database cannot reveal your bank accounts, insurance policies, real estate holdings, and the like—the less attractive a target you become. Anyone, or any family, with an above-average net worth can easily become the target of a frivolous lawsuit, a kidnapping or abduction, or even be the victim of an extortion plot.

In terms of privacy with a foreign policy, the extent of privacy is often determined by the jurisdiction where you establish your policy. For example, we can look at Switzerland and how the Swiss banks are governed by Swiss law. Neither a Swiss bank nor its employees may release client information to third parties without the written consent of the client. Only in the event of a criminal investigation—and it must be seen as a crime under Swiss law—can a bank be ordered by the Swiss authorities to release information. In many cases, these jurisdictions will require that it be a "named" criminal investigation, simply meaning that civil lawyers or detectives cannot place a call to the insurance company and gain access to your information.

If you establish your policy in the right jurisdiction, the insurance company will operate under its own insurance privacy law and can release information to third parties only in the event of a criminal investigation. A simple Internet or database search will never reveal the first clue that you may have a policy offshore. And, if necessary, the legal authorities in that jurisdiction may step up to defend your privacy rights.

As you're probably aware, privacy and the idea of "secrecy" have curiously been thrust into the limelight as the financial crisis started unraveling on American shores. In early 2009, the IRS demanded that the Swiss bank UBS reveal the names and information of all 52,000 American clients. UBS resisted, ultimately yielding the names of just a few thousand clients who were already the target of named criminal investigations. However, foreign private placement policies are easily reportable, so it is very easy to be compliant with U.S. government regulations. (See Chapter 4 for reporting requirements on each policy type.)

PEACE OF MIND FOR GENERATIONS

Few things meet with so much procrastination from so many people as writing a last will and testament or making arrangements for your estate.

But when signing the application for policy, you freely name the beneficiary(s) in the event of your death. No "power of-attorney," last will, or certificate of inheritance will be necessary for payments to be made. Beneficiaries get immediate access to the funds as the insurer pays out according to their instructions.

You may also determine when the payout should take place (e.g., not before the beneficiary has reached a certain age) or whether payments should be staggered out over time. If the beneficiary clause was not made irrevocable, you may adjust or change the designation at any given time.

TRANSPARENCY OF FEES AND EXPENSES

One negative point about annuities has centered on hidden—and often high—fees that were built into the U.S. policies. Rather than telling the investor up front about the involved fees, the insurance industry hides the fees in different ways or by creating high penalty fees that many investors triggered. For example, it is not uncommon to find that a U.S. annuity has a surrender fee of 7 to 8 percent. This means that when you go to take out your money, the surrender fee comes off the top before you get paid. Also, many insurance companies invest the money in their own investment funds, so you never know what fees are being paid to that fund out of your policy. But the funds are there to turn a profit for the company, so rest assured you are being hit with fees in one form or another.

With foreign private placement policies, the fees are transparent, so you know what you will pay to set up the policy as well as any ongoing fees. Typically, there is an entrance fee that is established when you create the policy. The entrance fee is either charged up front or charged over a five-year period. There are also annual policy administration fees that are paid to the insurance company, and an ongoing asset management fee that is paid to the adviser who is managing your account. These fees are established at the onset, so nothing is hidden from view. Also, the fees are based on the total amount in the policy, so they will be a higher percentage on smaller accounts and a lower percentage on larger accounts.

FROM MEAGER BEGINNINGS, THE MODERN INSURANCE POLICY THRIVES

The global insurance companies are in the catbird seat. They work in most, if not all, major world markets, and they see the developments happening around us. These companies are also in the unique position of catering to clients from multiple countries. Their lawyers and advisers are continually looking for opportunities to develop new products that will allow them serve even more nationalities. They are light years away from the insolated U.S. financial firms. They are truly on the cutting edge of the financial front line.

There are currently over a dozen different variations of private placement policies. Plus, most of these policies are super-flexible, so they can be tailored to properly fit each investor, whether they are Russian, Canadian, Norwegian, or American.

In the following chapter, we discuss the top three policies that are well suited for the American investor based on IRS compliance and reporting regulations. We are confident that you will be impressed when you learn how these policies accomplish so many of the investment and protection requirements facing our generation today.

CHAPTER 4

FINDING THE RIGHT POLICY TO MEET YOUR FINANCIAL GOALS AND SECURE YOUR PEACE OF MIND

As we've discussed in previous chapters, we are all facing new and potentially more damaging threats to our wealth. It's hard to know what the biggest risk will be. For some of you, it may be the threat of a lawsuit from a patron or tenant who has a slip-and-fall accident on your property. For others, it might be watching your retirement portfolio lose value due to inflation and declining purchasing power of the U.S. dollar.

We've touched on a few ways you can diversify and protect your investment accounts: using an offshore bank account, a trust, and, in some cases, an offshore LLC. Each of these tools offers a host of benefits, but none of those offer you a complete solution the way an annuity can.

Now we delve into the nuts and bolts of the different types of offshore policies available today so that you can see how these policies can help you create an insured portfolio, giving you and your money easy and direct access to the global markets.

This chapter contains some powerful information—the kind of information that people pay thousands of dollars for in the private offices of law firms and prestigious family offices. We are sharing it on these pages in a basic and easy-to-understand format so that more and more hardworking people just like you can learn how to put these types of solution to work for you. Now, the details we are going to share may not be riveting *bestseller* material, but neither is the user's manual for a Porsche 911 Turbo. But if you promise to grab an extra cup of coffee and roll up your sleeves, we promise to show you a one-stop solution that can solve virtually all of your needs as a twenty-first-century saver and investor.

THE TOP THREE SOLUTIONS FOR TWENTY-FIRST-CENTURY INVESTORS

In the next few pages, we take a detailed look at three of the different types of policy options available to you. These policies are:

- Deferred variable annuities (DVAs)
- Variable universal life policies (VULs)
- Frozen cash value policies (FCVs)

To get started, we will give you a synopsis of each policy. We will explain how it works, the basic benefits and disadvantages, and the U.S. reporting requirements involved with each. We'll also review a few real-world case studies for each type of policy, so you can see how these policies work. Plus, it is our hope that you'll recognize yourself in one of the stories and be able to see firsthand how the policy was created to solve the challenges.

Remember to keep in mind as you read that each type of policy is designed around a set of benefits found in existing laws and regulations. Remember the benefits of each policy and how the benefits are created. This will make easier it for you to see the differences between the three types.

POLICY 1: THE DEFERRED VARIABLE ANNUITY

Of all the different policy types we discuss in this chapter, the offshore DVA offers the greatest flexibility and is the most popular of the three policies. Because of this, we will spend a bit more time on the DVA since it can be used in a vast majority of situations and for a variety of people.

Indeed, the remaining two policies we discuss—the VUL and the FCV—are basically specialized insurance policies. They're built to serve a more specific purpose for a particular group of individuals; however, the structure will be relatively similar.

Let's start by highlighting a few different scenarios where the DVA would be a perfect fit:

- *If you're planning for your retirement.* The deferred variable annuity is an ideal solution for both personal and private pension. This policy allows you to invest and protect your money abroad with no negative tax consequences during the term of your policy. As we discussed in Chapter 2, U.S. tax laws and regulations enforced by the Securities and Exchange Commission make it difficult for a U.S. investor to directly invest in the global securities markets without undesirable tax issues or dramatically higher cost. However, the offshore DVA is one of the easiest and most efficient ways for investors to participate in international equities markets and benefit from tax deferral on the growth of those investments. It's a powerful combination that gives you the opportunity to diversify your portfolio without reporting headaches and hassles and allows you to be U.S. tax compliant in a simple way. In addition, it is one of the only ways to invest in foreign mutual funds without negative tax consequences.

  By reinvesting tax-deferred growth, and allowing the saving to compound over the course of several years, your policy could outpace comparable alternatives. In addition, your investment universe will be wide open to financial products you will not find here at home. Plus, you have the ability to denominate your policy in the foreign currency of your choice, meaning that you are not limited to the U.S. dollar. If you consider that an annuity established in 1971 and denominated in Swiss francs or even the Japanese yen would be worth at least three times more than one denominated in U.S. dollars.

The DVA also offers you peace of mind, knowing that you can enjoy full liquidity at any time. This allows you to withdraw money from the policy whenever you need it.

- *If you're looking for tax-deferred growth.* The tax deferral offered by the offshore variable annuity allows you to grow your account without paying tax until you take a distribution. While none of us can begin to guess what the future U.S. income tax rates will be, the strategy here is that many of you may be in lower tax brackets later in life when your active income is at a much lower level.

- *If you're looking for robust asset protection.* If you have any concerns that your wealth may make you a target in the wake of the ever-increasing "who can I sue" mentality in the United States, the DVA makes a great shield. With some customization of the policy, it is possible for the policy to become "judgment proof." Creditors will not be able to attach the contract, and you cannot be forced to assign the future benefit of the policy to such a creditor.

- *If you're looking for an easy, straightforward solution without having to permanently incur fees from lawyers and tax advisers.* You read that right. You'll need to consult the proper professionals in order to make your final decision, to set up your policy, and to make sure your plan is compliant with all applicable U.S. tax laws. But once your policy is in place, it requires only a minimal amount of maintenance on your part. Of course, you will need to file the appropriate tax forms each year (more on the details of proper tax reporting later), and we recommend that you keep an eye on changing tax laws. However, you will not need constant supervision from an army of professionals, which is often the case with an offshore trust.

- *If you plan on leaving the United States and giving up your citizenship.* Let us stop here for a moment to point out that it is a rare few that will consider giving up their citizenship and leaving the United States for good. But that number, however small, is starting to grow. According to a series of Zogby polls commissioned by New Global Initiatives between 2005 and 2007,[1] nearly 10 million U.S. households were "somewhat seriously" contemplating relocating abroad to "determined" to move abroad. Not all, of course, will give up their citizenship, but this number shows that more people than ever before are considering an escape plan. After all, these are tumultuous times for countries, economies, and governments alike. So it couldn't possibly hurt to have an exit strategy even if you never pull the trigger.

If this idea appeals to you, here is how the policy can be an effective strategy. Once you complete the expatriation process and once your U.S. tax liability ends, you may cancel the DVA and cash out tax free depending on the tax regulations in the country where you live at the time. Many expats relocate to countries with low or no taxes, and thus they are able to stretch the value of the policy quite far.

- *If you wish for your heirs to have immediate access to funds when you pass away.* With a DVA, upon the death of the insured, the money in the policy is distributed to the beneficiaries without having to go through probate or any other review process. This is a very important benefit if your heirs depend on a regular income stream to support themselves.

The Simple Setup of the DVA

Now that we've highlighted a few examples of the type of investor this type of policy might be well suited for, let's dig a bit deeper into how the policy is structured and funded.

The investor transfers the money to the insurer, and the insurer opens a *segregated subaccount* (more on this in a moment) with a specific bank (see Figure 4.1).

The investor selects an approved investment adviser or agrees to an investment strategy, and the money is invested accordingly by the adviser. The cash value of your policy will always be equal to the value of the underlying assets in the account minus any outstanding fees (see Figure 4.2).

As the underlying assets in the policy account grow or decline, the cash value of your policy grows or declines as well. Depending on your particular investment strategy, your money may be invested in stocks, international bonds, mutual funds, precious metals, and/or

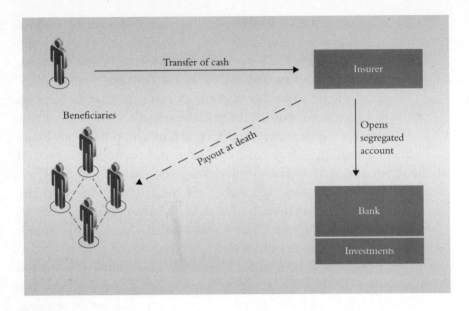

Figure 4.1 The Simple Setup of a Deferred Variable Annuity
Source: NMG International.

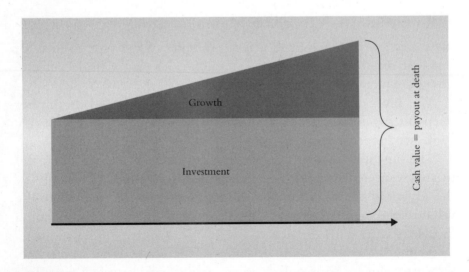

Figure 4.2 Deferred Variable Annuity
Source: NMG International.

foreign currencies. Technically, these holdings can be sold at any time, so the policy offers quick liquidity. Full withdrawals from the policy can be made on a case-by-case basis or at regular intervals, such as on a quarterly or biannual basis.

In many cases, you'll also have the option to convert your variable annuity to an immediate-starting fixed annuity, so you may receive guaranteed income payments for life. The ability to lock in guaranteed payments offers an additional layer of personal comfort. You will know that your financial payments are safe and can be relied on to be a protected source of regular, secure income for as long as you need it.

Given that these policies can be easily denominated in foreign currencies, you would have the ability to receive your income payments in a higher-yielding currency and convert the payments into U.S. dollars for your living expenses. This could generate a nice potential boost in income and remove some of the potential risks of U.S. inflation given the government's current deficit levels.

Also, when you pass away, the entire cash value of the DVA policy will be paid to your designated beneficiaries, according to your instructions. The policies can be distributed to multiple beneficiaries, including charities or other legal entities such as trusts.

Additional Protection for Heirs after You're Gone

The variable annuity policy offers an additional layer of protection for your beneficiaries to make sure your loved ones are taken care of properly. You would be amazed at how many family members are ill prepared to receive financial payouts. How family members will handle the distributions is always one of the top concerns when investors begin to focus seriously on creating an estate plan. With the flexibility of the DVA, when you create the policy, you have the option to add an arbiter to your policy. The arbiter is a third party—normally an attorney, an adviser, or a person that you trust, such as a family member. You can give the arbiter you select specific rights to ensure that your wishes are carried out after you pass on. For example, you could request that no withdrawals be made from the policy without the approval of the arbiter. There are many plausible reasons why you may wish to do this.

The most obvious reason usually centers around how equipped you feel your beneficiaries will be to handle the money you are leaving to them. You may have worked hard, invested wisely, and built a comfortable cushion for your family. However, your children, spouse, or parents may not be ready—or able—to handle that money responsibly. In some families, one child may be financially responsible while another one is the proverbial "wild child" who would rapidly squander his or her share of the policy distribution. This is where the arbiter can step in on your behalf and ensure that your wishes are carried out. Another situation where an arbiter can be useful concerns the payouts from a policy. Say that your children are the beneficiaries of your policy; however, you don't wish for them to receive any money from the policy until they reach a certain age, such as 18 or 21 years old. In this case, the arbiter would make the investment decision for the policy from the time of your death until the time that your children are old enough to receive their first payout. At that point, the arbiter could continue to oversee the investment decisions, or that responsibility could pass on to one of your children.

Another example where an arbiter is useful is if you would like the payouts to your beneficiaries to be made over a specific period of time rather then distributed all at once. This is not an uncommon request. Some people wish to see their children reach certain milestones in life before a distribution from the policy is made; for some, it may be marriage, having a child, or a grandchild's graduating from college. In this case, the arbiter could be given the right to make the decision on how much should be paid out and if the payments should be adjusted to inflation. Also, the arbiter could be given the authority to allow distributions to be taken in the event of something unexpected.

Finally, yet of great importance, is the arbiter's ability to prevent you from being forced to make a withdrawal from the policy while under duress. As discussed in Chapter 3, one of the great asset protection aspects of this policy is that once the policy has been in effect for more than one calendar year, the policy cannot be subject to creditor claims or legal judgments. However, should a situation arise where someone got a judgment against you and tried to coerce you into taking a distribution from the policy against your wishes, the arbiter could block it. You could contact the insurance company and demand a payment, but the arbiter would know that you were doing so only under duress and, thus, would say no. In this case, the insurance company would not be able to make the distribution to you because it would be in violation of the policy.

As you can see, the role of the arbiter is very flexible and can be defined in many ways, based on your wishes. It is important to clearly define the role you wish the arbiter to play and to set up this relationship carefully in cooperation with the adviser.

The Finer Points of the Offshore Variable Annuity

First, you probably noticed the segregated subaccounts at the heart of the DVA. Their primary function in U.S. annuities is to allow investors to engage in tax-deferred investing for retirement in amounts greater than permitted by individual retirement or 401(k) plans. These accounts are generally separated from the other insurance policies and other bank accounts so that your money is not commingled.

This offers a greater degree of protection if the insurance company or the bank should suffer or fail. Depending on the jurisdiction, each policy has a separate segregated account, and in the unlikely event that the insurance company should declare bankruptcy, the policy and its underlying account are segregated from the insurer's assets. This is very important for investor's peace of mind. This is just another benefit that allows twenty-first-century savers and investors to feel secure when investing overseas. We talk more about the various jurisdictions recommend to establish such policies in Chapter 5.

Also, take note of the cash value illustration in Figure 4.2. With a DVA, the cash value of the policy is always equal to the policy's "surrender value," or the payout that will be rendered upon surrender of the policy or death. For example, if the cash value of Policy A is $500,000, then that is the amount that will be paid out when the policy is terminated or upon the death of the policy creator.

That's a key distinction between the DVA and the remaining two policies we cover. The variable universal life policy, for example, incorporates life coverage, which functions very similarly to traditional life insurance, with which you're probably already familiar. As such, the cash value and the surrender value are often different. And as its name implies, the frozen cash value policy "freezes" the cash value of the policy at the original principal, with investment growth added to the surrender value of the policy. If any of this sounds complicated right now, don't worry. We cover these policies in depth later in the chapter.

There is another point we want to make that is relative to all three policies. There are no legal issues surrounding U.S. citizens purchasing foreign annuities as long as it is done properly, like most things in life. In order to make sure you are following the right path, here are a few important points to consider before you move forward.

You should create your policy well before you have a problem. If you have already become the target of a lawsuit or any other type of legal proceeding, it will be too late to form a policy and expect it to offer you asset protection. Also, you must be able to show that the money you plan to place within the policy is from a reputable source, such as savings, investment income, a pension, or the sale of home. It's important that the source of the funds be disclosed so it is clear you have nothing to hide.

And, finally, if you wish to purchase a foreign policy, you must do so abroad when you are outside of the United States. This is important in order to comply with terms and jurisdictional control over the policies.

Understanding U.S. Tax and Reporting Requirements

When you purchase a DVA policy, you must file IRS Form 720 (Appendix B-6) and pay a 1 percent excise tax on the premium paid to the foreign insurer. The federal excise tax is imposed by the U.S. government, and the payment is made to them (Appendix B-7).

The excise tax is applicable only when the person insured in the policy is a U.S. citizen. If a foreign family member is the insured, the excise tax will not be required. This situation may sound rare, but there are cases of naturalized U.S. citizens creating a DVA and making their parent or sibling who has not emigrated to the United States the insured party.

During the entire term of the policy, your investment gains will not trigger any payable U.S. taxes, and the asset manager handling the investments may freely buy and sell new securities as he or she sees fit. Depending on your policy, you may have the ability to switch between asset managers and into different investment strategies without triggering any tax liability.

Tax liabilities come into play when the money is paid out during the policyholder's lifetime, or to the designated beneficiaries in the event of the policyholder's death. At the time of the payment, the investment gains will be taxed at the ordinary income tax rate of the person receiving the distribution. It is important to note that when distributions are made, the growth portion of the policy will be paid out first. However, once that has been paid out, the return of principal will be paid income tax free. At present, U.S. ordinary income tax rates range from 10 percent to 35 percent.

If the person receiving the distribution payments is a beneficiary of the policy, the distribution will be subject to U.S. income taxes and possibly estate taxes, depending on the size of the total estate.

The strategy of the policy is to draw only as much money from the policy as you really need, and only at a time when your income tax bracket is relatively lower. The nature of the DVA gives you the flexibility you need to make specific plans and optimize your withdrawal plans based on your own personal tax situation.

Given the straightforward nature of the policies, knowing when to pay the due taxes and knowing how much to pay is quite simple. Your local CPA or accountant could easily assist you if needed.

While you may legally withdraw money from the policy at any time, once you reach the age of 59½, you may withdraw money from the policy whenever you need it without a tax penalty. Should you need to make a withdrawal prior to that age, you would face a tax penalty of 10 percent for making an early withdrawal. This penalty exists because the true benefit of the tax deferral is to help you save for your retirement so that you have enough money to live on comfortably in your later years. The IRS does not want these types of policies to be used for short-term tax deferral. However, should you have the misfortune of becoming disabled and unable to work before the age of 59½, you would be able to take distributions from your policy without paying any tax penalty.

To make a DVA compliant under U.S. law, a series of different rules must be met and followed. When you purchase a foreign variable annuity, you must also make sure that the insurer or broker you work with has done their homework. You should ask if the policy they are offering has been reviewed and approved by a licensed U.S. tax attorney. If you wish, you may also request a personal legal opinion for your own policy. You may request this opinion from the insurer or the broker, but be aware that this will be done at your own cost. Legal opinions can range in cost from $10,000 to $50,000 depending on the complexity of the policy. Most of the time, the legal opinion on the type of policy and its uses is enough to give you confidence that the solution is compliant.

Main Rules for Tax Deferral

Since tax deferral is such a key benefit for the DVA, let's take a moment to review in detail the different investment requirements your policy must meet in order to enjoy tax deferral under U.S. law.

First, it's important for you to understand that foreign variable annuities are not automatically set up for the investment assets to grow tax deferred. The IRS has created a clear set of rules and regulations that must be followed in order for the policy to qualify for tax deferral. It's critical that your policy be established appropriately before you start to invest.

Without being *too* technical about it, we are outlining what you should know and understand about the most important rules for a variable annuity to qualify for tax deferral.

One of the first and most important rules is that you, as the investor, cannot have control over the investments in the policy. In order to qualify for the tax deferral, it is vital that the underlying investments in the policy are considered to be owned by and under the direct control of the insurance company and not you, as the owner of the policy. In the same way that you wouldn't call Geico, for example, and advise them on how you'd like to invest the premiums you've paid for your car insurance, you shouldn't be in direct control of how the underlying investments of your variable annuity are managed.

As with other types of insurance and annuities, the owner of the policy has no control—direct or indirect—over the actual management of the investments or the selection of the investments in the contract aside from the choice of specific portfolios or funds offered by the insurance company to similar buyers of such contracts but not offered to the general public.

So, while you cannot tell the insurance company which investments to buy, you are allowed to decide on the type of investment strategy you want the policy to follow. These strategies are rather general in nature. For example, you can determine if you want the funds invested conservatively, with moderate risk, or aggressively. Also, the insurance company, as beneficial owner of the policy, is permitted to appoint an independent investment adviser to manage your account. Most insurance companies will tell you which advisers have been approved by them and will allow you to give them input as to which adviser you wish to manage your account.

So you may review the list, speak to a few of the advisers, and decide you like Matt Stover and Raymond Lewis. You could share your preference with the insurance company, and they could then appoint one or both of the advisers, depending on the size of your policy, to manage the investments.

The second rule that must be followed to ensure that your DVA receives tax-deferred treatment is that the policy must meet the IRS investment diversification rules. In order to qualify for favorable tax treatment, the policy must satisfy the following diversification requirements:

- No more than 55 percent of the value of the total assets of the account is represented by any one investment.
- No more than 70 percent of the value of the total assets of the account is represented by any two investments.
- No more than 80 percent of the value of the total assets of the account is represented by any three investments.
- No more than 90 percent of the value of the total assets of the account is represented by any four investments.

The rationale behind this rule is to protect the individual investor so that an adviser couldn't just limit a policy to one investment, putting your assets at risk for a crash or correction of that one investment. But there is another reason as well.

As you can imagine, there are always people who try to push the boundaries of what's allowable and what is not. The IRS diversification rule, by the way it has been designed, makes it impossible to wrap a publicly available fund, such as a mutual fund or hedge fund, in an annuity in order to circumvent the tax that you would normally pay if you invested in the funds directly. The tax deferral is a powerful investment tool when used properly.

You may have noticed that in regards to the first rule—investors may not have any direct control over investments—the rules are very strict and they are extremely clear. And since tax-deferred growth is such a major advantage for DVAs, you want to be certain that your plan is well within the letter of the law. But in reality, all this rule says is that you can't manage your own annuity like it's a broker-age account. You can't sign a policy contract that orders your insurer to purchase 5,000 shares of IBM on dividend reinvestment and still expect tax deferral.

That being said, you'll still have access to an immense variety of investments that wouldn't be available to you otherwise. And in our experience, the world's premier offshore financial centers offer more than enough variety of investment strategies and profiles to satisfy everyone's personal investment profile.

In fact, each offshore insurance company screens hundreds of top asset managers and select the very best to manage their policies. This gives you an enormous benefit as you gain access to top investment professionals that you would not probably be able to do on your own. If you are like most people, not only would it be nearly impossible to know where to start, but it would be amazingly time consuming as well. The majority of these managers are from Europe, the United Kingdom, and Asia. They have a wealth of knowledge of the global markets and can bring a fresh investment perspective to your portfolio.

Of course, there are other additional criteria for a variable annuity to qualify for U.S. tax deferral. But they're more technical in nature, often arising in the form of various legal opinions rather than clear rules and regulations. This is just another reason it's important to have a qualified legal opinion when setting up your policy.

If you decide to invest in a foreign variable annuity, you must make sure that the broker and the insurer are experienced with U.S. clients and have done the necessary legal homework. Ideally, as mentioned earlier, you should request a legal opinion for your own policy. This will increase your purchasing costs, but keep in mind that you won't need to permanently engage legal professionals and tax advisers dur-ing the lifetime of your policy. Also, depending on the size of your policy, it may be worth it.

Annual U.S. Reporting Requirements for the
Annuity Policy

Now, with respect to the annual U.S. reporting requirements for
the policies, there are varying opinions. Some very highly reputable
U.S. law firms believe that the only form that needs to be filed with
the IRS at the time the policy is created is IRS Form 720. After
that, no other annual form must be filed. However, other highly
respected firms believe that you should file form TDF 90-22.1,
(Appendix B-8) a U.S. Treasury form that requires taxpayers to dis-
close all foreign financial accounts that have a separate or combined
value over $10,000.

We don't believe in taking *any* unnecessary risks, so should you
choose to set up a DVA policy, we recommend spending a few extra
minutes each year to file the TDF 90-22.1 form. Since the IRS language is rather gray and the lawyers are split on what's best, we feel
you should err on the side of caution.

In March 2010, a new compliance act was signed into law: the
Foreign Account Taxpayer Compliance Act. It was neatly tucked
into a jobs bill, cleverly entitled the Hiring Incentives to Restore
Employment (HIRE) Act, H.R. 2847. The HIRE Act imposes much
more stringent reporting and information exchange requirements on
foreign financial institutions and we believe its main effect will be
to make U.S. citizens even more unattractive to offshore providers.
However, the act does not change Americans' access to annuities or
other offshore financial opportunities, but it would require a bit more
paperwork when reporting these accounts. However, most portions
of this law do not go into effect until 2012–2013 and very well may
be changed or repealed by then.

Now let's take a look at a case study to see how the DVA works in
a "real-life" situation.

*Case Study: Deferred Variable Annuity—Jerry the Bachelor Gives a Helping
Hand to Mom*

Jerry was an energetic bachelor who built a substantial fortune in the
world of investment banking and spent most of his free time climbing
mountains and jumping out of airplanes. He was a real risk taker with
a strong sense of adventure.

Jerry never married and never had any children. His only real concern was his mother. His mom was a widow in her early 70s, and she was financially dependent on Jerry. Jerry wanted to make sure that if something happened to him on one of his exotic adventures or by the hand of fate, his mother would still be financially secure and receive an annual income of about $50,000 for the rest of her life. Jerry also had another concern. He was worried that she might be an easy target for scam artists or unreliable advisers, so he didn't necessarily want to give her control over the money. It became pretty clear that Jerry would need a variable annuity policy for his mother.

The goals of the policy were:

- Jerry should keep control over the assets as long as he's alive.
- If he dies, there should be no delay for the mother to receive payments—no waiting periods, no probate; the income should go directly to her.
- The money should remain invested in a conservative portfolio, and the capital should stay intact in the hands of a capable and financially educated individual while the mother receives her income.
- The payments should also be flexible, so they could be adjusted if Jerry's Mom needed more money in the future for any reason.

Here is how the solution was created:

First was determining the amount of money that Jerry would need to invest in the policy to get his mother a set amount of yearly income without touching the principal. Jerry wanted his mother to receive $50,000 of yearly income. Based on prevailing market conditions and professional experience, it was reasonable to expect a 5 percent net annual return from a conservative portfolio. So Jerry needed to fund the policy with approximately $1 million in order to secure his mother's income and not touch any of the principle.

So a deferred variable annuity was created with the following parameters (see Figure 4.3):

- Policyholder: Jerry
- Succeeding policyholder in the event of the policyholder's death: Jerry's mother
- Person insured: Jerry's mother

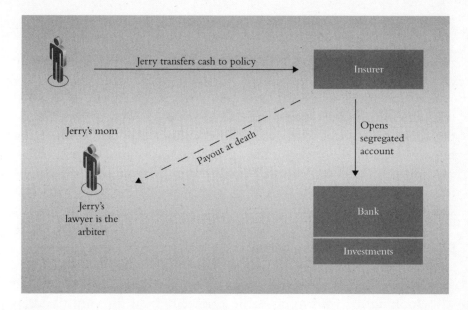

Figure 4.3 DVA Created for Jerry to Provide for His Mother
Source: NMG International.

- Beneficiary at death of the insured: Jerry
- Arbiter: Jerry's lawyer

Choosing Jerry as the policyholder ensured that he would keep the assets under his control for as long as he lived. He could increase or surrender the policy at any time. If he happened to pass away early or unexpectedly, his mother was assigned to be the succeeding policyholder. At that same time, the policy would start paying out an income to Jerry's mother, as set forth earlier.

In this case, the arbiter plays only a minor role. The arbiter is given the right to make decisions with respect to the investment strategy, to appoint asset managers, and to adjust income payouts to the mother, if appropriate. Should Jerry's mother pass away before he does, he has a few options. He could choose to receive the income payouts himself. Jerry could continue to control the policy, but he could change the beneficiary policy choosing to name a friend or a favorite charity. Or he could also opt to liquidate the policy. This is yet another example of the flexibility that these types of structures can offer.

POLICY 2: THE VARIABLE UNIVERSAL LIFE POLICY

As we mentioned briefly in the preceding section, the VUL is actually quite similar to a DVA with a few key exceptions.

You can think of a VUL as a middle ground between traditional life insurance and a cutting-edge DVA. With a VUL you will gain the same benefits of a traditional life insurance policy because the life coverage in this policy offers you a hedge against the risk of an unknown future. Plus, you will benefit from all the flexibility, liquidity, and asset protection of a DVA as is possible for your particular situation.

The VUL would be an appropriate solution for those who are looking for the following benefits:

- *If you want to save your wealth for the next generation.* If you are looking for your assets to be primarily held for your children or even your grandchildren, but you are concerned that you may need significant extra liquidity during your lifetime, the VUL may be useful. In this policy, the money grows tax free as long as it is in the policy and at death the policy will pay income tax free to the next generation. However, it will not pass to your beneficiaries' estate tax free. For this reason, if your main goal is to pass on money, a variable life policy may be better than a variable annuity. But, it goes without saying that the additional costs for the extra premiums for the life insurance coverage will eat up some of your profits. Therefore, if you may need the money during your lifetime, a DVA may be the better solution. This is especially true if you have any health issues that would prevent you from qualifying for the life coverage.
- *If you need a substantial amount of life insurance.* If you are looking to ensure that your heirs receive a large sum of money—larger than the cash value of your policy—when you pass away, this is the only policy that offers the option of adding additional funds. Some high-net-worth people find this policy ideal because the additional life coverage can be used to help their heirs pay the estate tax due upon their death. Having this additional money can prevent the family from having to sell assets in order to cover the tax bill. However, you must be insurable. This is a critical

point because in order to qualify for the insurance coverage, an extensive medical examination will be required.

As mentioned earlier, a VUL incorporates an element of traditional life insurance in a format similar to the DVA. But the similarities between a VUL and common American life insurance pretty much end right there.

That's because the strict laws governing life insurance in the jurisdictions you might utilize—for example, Liechtenstein or Switzerland—offer you a degree of security that simply can't be found in America. In Switzerland and Liechtenstein, life insurance has been big business for 160 years now. And in all that time—thanks to careful, client-friendly regulation—there hasn't been a single insurer to fail or declare bankruptcy.

Compare that to profit-hungry, unhinged American firms, and we are sure you'll see what we mean.

So the fact that you're getting life coverage with your policy isn't the real advantage. Rather, it's *where* you're getting that insurance that makes all the difference in the world. We discuss the various jurisdictions in greater depth in Chapter 5.

That being said, it is important to understand that, by incorporation, the life insurance and the way in which a VUL is constructed introduces a whole new set of regulations, tax laws, and reporting requirements to the equation. Many of the tax and reporting rules of the DVA still apply here, but we'll also talk about some additional features and requirements of this particular type of policy.

We'll cover those in a moment, but first let's review how this policy is created.

The Simple Setup of the VUL

Let's dig a bit deeper now to see how the policy is structured and funded. If the policy is structured to be a VUL, then the following main characteristics apply:

- The investor transfers money to the insurer.
- The insurer opens a segregated subaccount with a specific bank, and the money is invested and managed according to the agreed strategy.

- The cash value of your policy will always equal the value of the underlying account. This part is identical to the process to open and fund a variable annuity policy.

There is one very substantial difference between the ways in which the DVA and the VUL are executed. With a VUL, your beneficiaries receive a larger amount of money than the policy cash value upon death of the insured. In order to qualify as a VUL under the tax code, the policy must include a certain amount of life insurance coverage. We explain the details of the life coverage below, but Figure 4.4 shows how the life coverage comes into play.

As the underlying account grows, so does the cash value of the policy. Additionally, you still benefit from the full liquidity of the policy and, like the DVA, withdrawals can be made from the policy on a case-by-case or regular basis such as quarterly or biannually.

When the insured passes away, the entire cash value of the policy—plus the additional life coverage—will be paid to the beneficiaries, according to the specific wishes of the insured.

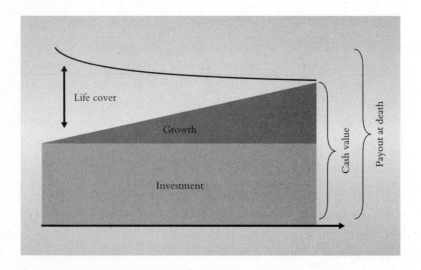

Figure 4.4 Variable Universal Life Policy
Source: NMG International.

The Finer Points of the VUL

In a very similar fashion to a variable annuity, the VUL has a seg-regated bank subaccount to invest the funds. Also similar to a DVA, the VUL gives you full liquidity, allowing you to withdraw or close the policy on your own schedule. However, there are two different ways a VUL can be funded, and they have slightly different tax implications.

A VUL can be created with a single premium payment, like the DVA, and have additional life coverage. If the premium is paid all at once, the VUL is considered to be a modified endowment contract (MEC).

The criteria for an MEC are defined under IRS code section 7702 (Appendix B-9), and it is dependent on an actuarial relationship between the premium payments and the death benefit. We will dis-cuss the impact on how the policy is taxed later.

The VUL can also be created by depositing multiple payments over a certain period of years, rather than with a single premium up front.

If the premium is paid into the VUL over a period of years and a number of other criteria are met, as outlined in IRS code section 7702, the policy is considered to be a non-MEC. This designation does change the way in which money may be withdrawn from the policy. Also, to be a VUL non-MEC policy, the policy must meet the require-ments for the seven-pay test, which is also part of IRS code section 7702. This is a rather complicated test (Appendix B-10).

For starters, it has nothing to do with the actual number of pre-mium payments. The test uses actuarial calculations in conjunction with the amount of the policy to determine the limits on the total amount you can pay into your policy in the first seven years of its existence. Specifically, the seven-pay test is designed to discour-age premium schedules that would result in a paid-up policy before the end of that seven-year period. That said, we have seen cases where the full premium amount has been paid into the policy in the first five to seven years, and others where it has taken over 25 years for the full premium to be paid into the policy. Because the seven-pay test involves actuarial calculations, there is no cut-and-dried answer to this. The VUL is a custom policy, and specific situations of each policy vary, based on the particular set of circumstances. These policies offer

very robust asset protection, investment diversification, and tax opti-
mization benefits; however, you must work with a professional.

Let's take a look at two case studies to see how these minor technical
differences can make a major real-life impact for the right investor.

*Case Study: A VUL MEC—Alfred Needs Cash to Help His Daughter
Cover Future Estate Taxes*

Alfred Steiner was a Swiss American who had been living in Los
Angeles, California, for nearly 40 years. Alfred started his own shoe
factory in the early 1970s, and he still owned the company in late
2009. He was 61 years old, widowed, and had one daughter who was
in her late 20s. Over the years, Alfred had purchased several proper-
ties, worked hard to pay off all the mortgages, and now he owned
the assets free and clear. He was a very cautious man, and his living
expenses were rather modest considering his substantial wealth. Even
though he was in excellent health, Alfred wanted to ensure that he
could put away a portion of his money—yet keep enough on hand
for his future expenses—in a safe and tax-efficient manner so that it
could easily be passed on to his daughter when he died. Thanks to
Alfred's success in the real estate market, he was expecting that the
daughter would face a substantial estate tax bill, and he wanted to
make sure that she had enough cash available upon his death that she
would not be forced to sell any of the assets.

Since he was used to making all the financial decisions, Alfred was
not prepared to give up any control over his money, plus he wanted to
be sure that he had access to the money in the policy in the event that
something unexpected occurred.

The goals of the policy for Alfred were:

- He wanted to keep control over the assets as long as he was alive.
- He wanted to leave a sustainable nest egg for his young daughter, so he needed a policy with tax-efficient growth for the
  long-term.
- He wanted his daughter to have quick access to the funds in the
  event of his death.
- Since Alfred's estate would contain a large share of valuable real
  estate, his daughter would need an increased payout at his death
  to pay the estate taxes.

Here is how a solution was created to meet his goals.

Alfred already had sizeable savings, so he was able to fund the VUL with a single premium payment (MEC). After looking at Alfred's entire financial picture and determining how much cash he would need during his lifetime so that he would not need to make a withdrawal from this policy, the VUL MEC was funded with a single premium of $15 million. An additional layer of life coverage was added to his policy. The amount of life coverage is determined by different actuarial formulas; however, the IRS has established a minimum threshold of coverage that must be included under IRS code section 7702. This government-established threshold takes into consideration your age and the total cash value of your policy. Based on Alfred's situation, as stated, his initial premium payment into the policy was $15 million; however, at his death the expected payout was approximately $41 million (Appendix B-11).

This particular policy was created using the following parameters (see Figure 4.5):

- Policyholder: Alfred
- Person insured: Alfred
- Beneficiary: Alfred's daughter
- Arbiter: None

Since Alfred was in excellent health, and due to his relatively young age, it was possible to insure him and thus set up a single-premium VUL. The result would be that all future growth in the policy would remain without any tax consequences for as long as Alfred did not withdraw any money, which was not his intention. If something unexpected happened in the future, as the policyholder, Alfred could withdraw money at any time. Much like the DVA, any growth on the policy would be paid out first, and he would need to pay U.S. income tax on that amount.

However, upon his death, the entire payout to his daughter would take place separately from the ordinary estate, so it would be very quick and avoid probate. The investment growth, as well as the principal investment of $15 million, would pass on to her income tax free. Of course, there would be estate tax to be paid. But since the policy had a substantial amount of life coverage involved, there would be substantial cash available to pay for the overall estate tax.

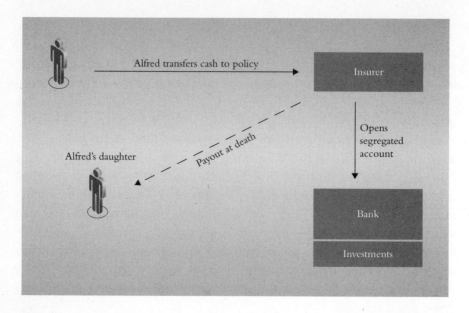

Figure 4.5 VUL Created for Alfred to Help with Estate Taxes
Source: NMG International.

It goes without saying that this type of policy, with the large amount of life coverage, could be set up only because Alfred was in excellent health; otherwise, it would have been impossible to find a company to insure him. Also, we must point out that the cost for the life coverage is pretty substantial, and it will erode some of the annual returns. If Alfred's primary goal had been to access the money during his lifetime, rather than pass it on to his daughter, a DVA would have been a better alternative because there would have been additional expenses for the life coverage and the investment returns could be optimized.

Case Study: A VUL Non-MEC—John Wants to Pass Wealth to His Children but Needs Flexibility in Funding His Policy

John was 55 years old and had built a substantial fast-food franchise. His business had finally reached a point where he was able to draw a substantial income every year; in fact, it was far more than he needed. John wanted to make sure that some of the money could be set aside for his three children, who ranged in age from 18 to 27. His goal was to leave them with substantial cash so they could enjoy life, but also so they could pay the estate taxes when he died without being forced to liquidate assets or, worse, to sell the business.

John was still young, and he wanted the control and the flexibility to withdraw funds from the policy should his life change in the course of the next several years. It was very likely that he would need to access some of the funds in the future if he wanted to expand the business further. Furthermore, while his business was doing very well at the moment, John needed flexibility with respect to the "annual savings" since his income stream was fluctuating.

The goals of the policy for John were:

- Tax-efficient growth on the money he invested. Due to his young age and his three kids, he wanted the money to grow as much as possible.
- He wanted to keep control over the assets as well as access to them in case he decided to reinvest in his business.
- He needed flexibility in paying the premium since he was depending on his current income stream and not pulling from a lump sum already established.
- Since his estate would be subject to a large estate tax bill, he needed to ensure that his family would have an increased cash payout upon his death.

Here is how the VUL non-MEC policy was a solution to his needs:

This specific type of policy allowed John to pay annual premiums on the insurance policy. With this kind of policy, he enjoyed a great amount of flexibility with respect to the annual premiums. The actual amount of premium and frequency of payments would affect the accumulation value in his policy and the amount and duration of insurance coverage. Of course, there is a certain limitation to the flexibility of the premiums. For example, there was a maximum amount that could be paid in at any one time. If the maximum premium was exceeded, then the policy no longer qualified as a non-MEC policy. The policy must meet the requirements for the seven-pay test according to IRS code section 7702. This is a rather complicated test.

For starters, it has nothing to do with the actual number of premium payments. The test uses actuarial calculations in conjunction with the amount of the policy to determine the limits on the total amount you can pay into your policy in the first seven years of its existence. Specifically, the seven-pay test is designed to discourage premium schedules that would result in a paid-up policy before the end of that seven-year period.

This particular policy was created using the following parameters (see Figure 4.6):

- Policyholder: John
- Person insured: John
- Beneficiaries: John's three children
- Arbiter: None

As long as John is alive, he can withdraw from the principal if he needs to without triggering any income tax. This is because with VUL non-MEC policies, the principal comes out first. However, if

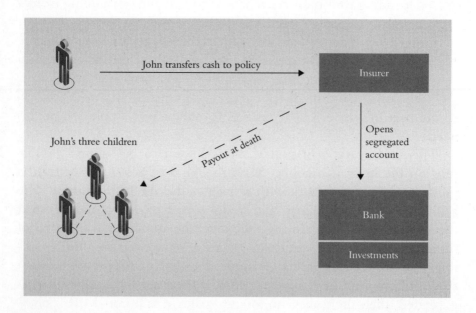

Figure 4.6 VUL Created for John and His Family

Source: NMG International.

John does not need any money, he can just let the policy grow until he dies. Upon his death, his children will receive a substantial amount of cash from the insurance company, which will be income tax free. This way, they can use the cash to easily pay off the estate tax, and they will still have money available for their personal needs.

Understanding the Tax and Reporting Requirements

Similar to the DVA, when you purchase the policy, you must file IRS Form 720 and pay a 1 percent excise tax on the premium paid to the foreign insurer. Please remember that the excise tax is applicable only where the insured person is a U.S. citizen.

During the entire term of the VUL, your investment gains will not be taxed, and the asset manager may freely adjust and rebalance the portfolio as they see fit without triggering any taxes. So to this point the tax treatments of the two policies we have review thus far are identical.

However, the tax differences between the VUL MEC and non-MEC and our original variable annuity arise when the value of the policy is being passed along to beneficiaries.

How the VUL policy is taxed at the time of the payout depends on whether the policy is considered to be an MEC. The criteria are defined under IRS code section 7702 (Appendix B-9), and it's basically dependent upon an actuarial relationship between the premium payments and the death benefit.

If the VUL policy is considered to be a non-MEC, then during his or her lifetime the owner can withdraw the amount of the premium paid into the policy tax free. In these types of policies, the principal is withdrawn first. Furthermore, loans can generally be made from this policy on a tax-free basis, even if they are in excess of the cumulative adjusted premium payments.

If correctly structured, the growth on the VUL non-MEC policy is not subject to income tax when it is paid to the beneficiaries upon the death of the insured. However, it is subject to estate taxes.

If the VUL policy is considered to be MEC, then during his or her lifetime the owner can make withdrawals from the policy; however, those withdrawals are subject to U.S. income tax because the *growth* on the investment comes out before the *principal*. In addition, such a distribution from a VUL MEC policy would result in an additional 10 percent penalty tax if the owner is younger than 59½ years of age.

In these ways, the tax situation of the VUL MEC policy is very similar to the DVA when money is withdrawn during the owner's lifetime. However, any payout that is made to the beneficiaries upon the death of the insured is fully income tax free, like the VUL non-MEC, but estate tax will need to be paid.

Here's a practical example of how these work: let's say you invest $1 million in a VUL MEC policy. This means that you will fund the policy all at one time, and your money will be invested according to the agreed investment strategy. Now, let's say that the policy has grown to $1,250,000 and you need $500,000 to purchase a house. You have two options: you can either make a withdrawal from the policy or take out a policy loan. The tax consequences will be the same either way.

Now, recall that your policy increased in value, so you had a gain of $250,000. If you decide to withdraw the $500,000 or take out a loan, you will need to pay income tax on the first $250,000 because it represents the growth on your original investment. The second $250,000 represents the return of your principal and is tax free. This is similar to the DVA.

The difference here is that distributions from a *non*-MEC policy are generally tax free up to the amount you originally invested. The same is true for any policy loans. This difference is because in the non-MEC policy the principal is withdrawn first, which does not trigger a taxable event. Only if you withdraw more than you originally invested will you be taxed on the growth portion of your withdrawal.

POLICY 3: THE FROZEN CASH VALUE POLICY

The frozen cash value policy (FCV) is a relatively new policy and is unknown to many people, especially when compared to its cousins, the DVA and the VUL. We want to point out that this policy is somewhat disputed in the marketplace, with some advisers feeling that this policy is too aggressive in the way in which it offers income tax–free distributions. We'll go into the details later; however, keep in mind that this special type of policy is offered by only a few specialized insurers, and it will be a good fit for only a very limited number of readers. Before making any type of financial decision, you should always work with a properly licensed tax attorney to ensure that you are compliant.

So how do you know if an FCV is right for you?

- If assets are primarily held for the next generation, and the money will not be needed during your lifetime
- If you don't need any additional life insurance to cover estate taxes or if you are uninsurable, as this type of policy requires no medical examination
- If you're primarily seeking protection and tax-free growth

As the name implies, the key attribute of an FCV is that the cash value of the policy remains frozen from the day you create the policy. This type of structure should highlight the fact that you, as the insured, own a policy and not the actual underlying investments. The cash value of that policy can be fixed for a predetermined period of time, as described in the language of the actual policy.

This type of policy offers liquidity, but one of the important factors is that the owner of the policy is limited to making withdrawals from the principal only and never the gains. This means that any withdrawals you make from an FCV can be done tax free. It does not offer the same flexibility as the DVA or the VUL because in this policy, you may never withdraw the gains on the investments during your lifetime.

Once the insured passes away, the cash value of the policy is adjusted to reflect the growth of the policy's underlying investment portfolio, and the funds are paid out according to the wishes of the insured.

The Simple Setup of an FCV

If you choose to create an FCV, you, as the investor, will transfer your money to the insurer. The insurer will open a segregated sub-account with a specific bank, and the money will be invested according to the agreed strategy. This is identical to the process to open and fund a DVA.

The cash value of your policy will be equal to the value of the underlying account, as long as that doesn't exceed the amount of the premium paid. So during your life, the cash value of the policy will never grow. Only when the insured passes away will the cash value include the entire value of the underlying account, including investment growth (see Figure 4.7).

Here's an example of how such a policy can be beneficial.

Case Study: An FCV—Elizabeth Wants to Leave a Legacy for Her Grandson and Nieces

Elizabeth Morgan is a charming and very classy lady from Arizona, in her early 60s. Her family is invested in the oil and gas business. Elizabeth wants to make sure that a large portion of her money is protected in case there are some legal threats made to her wealth. In addition, she wants her money to be able grow tax deferred and to be passed on to her grandson and three nieces in a tax-efficient way once she dies. Until then, she wants to keep control over the bulk of her money, and due to the young ages of her beneficiaries, she wants to ensure that someone will oversee the policy until they reach 21 years

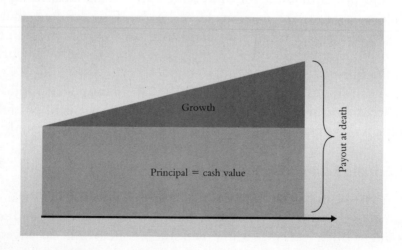

Figure 4.7 Frozen Cash Value Policy
Source: NMG International.

old. She does not plan to use any of this money for herself, but wants to have the flexibility to at least access some of it, if needed. Elizabeth has very high blood pressure and is not insurable.

The goal of this policy for Elizabeth is:

- To provide tax-efficient growth on the money she invested.
- To ensure she keeps control over the assets until her death.
- To provide a tax-optimized way to pass the wealth on to her heirs.

This particular policy was created using the following parameters (see Figure 4.8):

- Policyholder: Elizabeth
- Person insured: Elizabeth
- Beneficiaries: Elizabeth's grandson and three nieces
- Arbiter: Elizabeth's sister

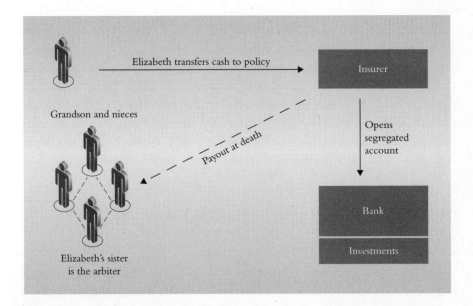

Figure 4.8 FCV Created for Elizabeth to Pass Wealth to Her Heirs

Source: NMG International.

Elizabeth is the perfect example of a client who would be looking for an FCV. With an FCV, she pays all the money into the policy at once in a single premium. All future growth on her premium will grow tax deferred, and upon her death the policy will be paid out income tax free to her grandson and her two nieces. (This is different than the variable annuity, where all distributions to beneficiaries are subject to U.S. income taxes.) During Elizabeth's lifetime she will have access to the premium that she paid into the policy, but not to the gains. Those will be paid out only at her death. Since the FCV does not include any life coverage, she does not need to pass a medical test.

Understanding the Tax and Reporting Requirements

Just like the other two types of policies, you'll have to file Form 720 and pay a 1 percent excise tax on the premium paid to the foreign insurer. During the entire term of the policy, there will be no taxable gain, since the cash value is frozen at the original amount and, as mentioned above, any withdrawals will be tax free since you're redeeming only principal.

As we mentioned at the beginning of this section, some advisers question the legality of this policy and feel it could be pushing the limit because of the payout upon the death of the insured is income tax free. Typically, only life insurance payments are made income tax free. And the FCV does not offer any type of life coverage. That said, there are a few legal opinions that support the income tax–free payments, and this policy is available on the market today. Nonetheless, we advise you speak to your own tax specialist to get a professional opinion.

INSURANCE POLICIES—THE GATEWAY TO STRESS-FREE GLOBAL INVESTMENTS

When looking for a way to protect your portfolio from ever-growing risks, such as greedy wealth predators or currency inflation risks at home, you don't have to look much farther that foreign insurance policies to find your solution. Not only do policies like the DVA offer a wide range of flexibility as to how the policy can pay out, but they also offer easy U.S. tax compliance, which is extremely important in these days of ever-growing government regulations.

The best way to determine the right policy for you is to decide what your goal is for the money you place in the policy. Are you looking to take regular payments from the policy when you retire? Or perhaps you are in a unique situation where you wish for your family to have extra cash available when you die to cover tax liabilities. The real value of these policies is that they can be customized in many ways to meet your long-term investment needs. It's easy to see why these policies are growing in popularity.

Another huge benefit to twenty-first-century savers and investors is that these policies allow you to select some of the finest asset managers from around the globe so that you can have the ability to participate in the truly international markets capitalizing on the opportunities, using a level of risk that you control. This saves you from the daunting task of trying to pick and choose the best international investments for your portfolio. In addition, the IRS-approved tax deferral of the growth of your policy means that your money can be invested in foreign mutual funds without any negative tax consequence. All of this is possible as long as the investment decisions are made by an asset manager and not by you directly.

These policies make it easy for you to receive regular payments for life, with the added benefit of being easily transferred to your family upon your death. This one-stop solution can be your gateway to stress-free international investments and estate planning.

CHAPTER 5

THE IMPORTANCE OF A JURISDICTION FOR YOUR INSURED PORTFOLIO— PLUS OUR TOP RECOMMENDATIONS

So far in this book, we've discussed the wealth threats we all face, the different international solutions, and the various ends to which you can use an offshore variable annuity and other similar policies, such as the variable universal life policy (VUL) or the more controversial frozen cash value policy (FCV).

Now that you have a solid grasp of how these policies work, it's important to understand the role that the jurisdiction in which your policy is created plays in the overall picture. This is the second most important decision you will need to make after you decide how a policy could work for your wealth needs.

This is where the rubber meets the road—it is where the possibilities become a reality. And the country you choose does make a difference when it comes to many aspects of the insurance policy. Much like any legal contract, the laws governing that contract are what can make or break its effectiveness. You can liken it to the difference in taste and overall experience between eating a steak at a roadside truck stop compared to a filet mignon from Smith & Wollensky's or New York Prime. Given the importance of these policies to your overall financial future, you shouldn't spare any expense in investment such as this one. Don't be impressed with some new, modern-sounding alternative that might seem to offer some kind of shortcut (lower costs, greater profits, etc.). Keeping your money safe is highly important; thus, you must be sure you're keeping your money with the best in the world.

In fact, there are just a scant few jurisdictions throughout the entire world and all its 256 countries that have what it takes to warrant your consideration as a home for your policy.

Why so few?

Well, you want to apply some exacting standards when shopping around for such a significant investment. Our selection criteria include:

- *Highest possible level of political and economic stability*. Most of us are old enough to remember at least hearing about the experience of foreign investors in President Noriega's Panamanian bank. In short, there was a regime change, Noriega was taken down, and all the funds in his bank were confiscated in the process. We can't stress enough the sensitivity you should have in choosing a home jurisdiction for your policy. When making such a careful and sizable investment, you shouldn't have to compromise. You should be relatively certain that the jurisdiction chosen—and its corresponding political regime—will be stable and in place for the duration of your policy. And an environment like this is what you find in Europe, where you can rely on the law to be stable and rely on things to change slowly and deliberately, rather than chaotically and unexpectedly. You want to be sure any jurisdiction you choose has a history of having a stable legal system and where processes and procedures work, and work well.
- *Built-in legal protection*. We're talking about asset protection and insurance secrecy laws, the kind of legal foundation that makes the benefits discussed in previous chapters possible in the first place. Peace of mind, when it comes to asset protection, is ultimately possible only with the firm backing of a proved legal system. The continent of Europe is a great example of this. After decades of wars and political instability, Europe developed into an area with strong and stable democracies, reflecting a learned respect for neighbors, property, ownership, and personal freedom.

- *Strong supervision and regulation.* This criterion might have you scratching your head, but it's surprisingly important. If a country has legal asset protection but little or no supervision over the institutions you're doing business with, then your money just isn't safe. Gravity causes planes to crash, and greed does the same to companies; it doesn't matter which country we're talking about. A skillful pilot can prevent a plane crash, and skillful regulators can keep the insurance industry humming along. In Switzerland, for example, supervision over insurers is and always has been very strict. As a result, there hasn't been a single failure in the history of the Swiss life insurance industry. Not one.
- *Tradition and incentive to protect privacy and respect property.* This final criterion is about the "big picture." In the world's countries, as you'll see momentarily, protection and quality are derived from a long tradition. It influences the mentality of those running the country and its companies. And in today's world of global connectivity, many of the world's financial havens realize that they have a simple incentive: maintain a clean track record of respecting privacy and property, and more foreigners will send you their money. The benefits of increased foreign business are often felt at the national level in these jurisdictions, which is especially important in democratic countries, where the electorate could potentially influence radical changes to the law.

Applying these criteria, we ended up with a relatively short list of possible homes for your new variable annuity. We then classified them further, dividing them into three levels reflecting their overall stability.

Level I: The Most Stable and the Most Proven
- Switzerland
- Liechtenstein
- Isle of Man
- Luxembourg

Level II: Not as Strong, Equally Stable—Secondary Candidates
- Republic of Ireland
- Cayman Islands

- Singapore
- Nevis
- Bermuda

Level III: Up-and-Coming Havens and Those with Flaws

- Brunei
- Seychelles
- Bahamas

As we said earlier, we believe that quality of the country you do business with is very important, and in this case, you get what you pay for. Here you are paying for years of stability, honest and well-tested legal systems, and proper regulatory supervision. We believe you should spare no expense.

Through years of experience and education, we've learned that—for the vast majority of you—that's going to mean Switzerland, Liechtenstein, the Isle of Man, or Luxembourg. These countries are the leaders in the insurance world and have been for years. However, there is evolution in this industry and, as such, other countries are doing their best to become proven stars.

So for the rest of the chapter, we're going to "divide and conquer" the preceding list.

For a few of the most relevant top candidates, we're going to take an in-depth look at what makes them tick, including taking a look at the country's history, its political establishment, and its insurance industry. For the secondary jurisdictions, we take a quicker look at the countries in brief, highlighting their benefits and weaknesses.

With regards to the third-level countries, we address them only briefly here. To be honest, while these countries are showing promise in the world of global finance, at the moment they don't have much of a track record. They're aggressive, to be sure, but they don't have the all-important traditions we mentioned earlier, nor are their regulatory bodies as well established. So their future is uncertain. For example, we *might* have considered Dubai an "up-and-coming haven," but after the grand Dubai World default in November 2009, we wouldn't advise considering it. Uncertainty is not something that should come into play when establishing a long-term wealth solution. There are too many other countries that can make the process worry free.

So let's get started.

LEVEL I JURISDICTIONS: THE MOST STABLE AND MOST PROVEN

Where better to start than a country known around the world for its unchallenged domination of global finance—Switzerland.

Switzerland: The Historic Home of Wealth and Tradition

Switzerland is our choice as the best all-around asset and financial haven in the world. (See Figure 5.1 for a map of Switzerland.) For centuries, it has acted as banker to the world, and in that role

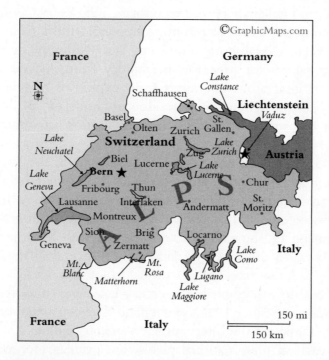

Figure 5.1   Map of Switzerland
Source: www.worldatlas.com.

has acquired a reputation for integrity and strict financial privacy. It is also a great place for the wealthy to reside. Switzerland may be neutral in politics, but it's far from flavorless. The fusion of German, French, and Italian ingredients has formed a robust national culture, and the country's Alpine landscapes have enough zing to reinvigorate the most jaded traveler. Goethe summed up Switzerland succinctly as a combination of "the colossal and the well ordered." You can be sure that your trains and letters will be on time. The tidy, just-so precision of Swiss towns is tempered by the lofty splendor of the landscapes that surround them. There's a lot more here than just trillions of dollars.

History and Overview

For many centuries, the Swiss have maintained more or less strict neutrality toward other countries, including those with which it shares a common border—France, Germany, Liechtenstein, Austria, and Italy. Isolated in the valleys of their Alpine redoubt, the various Burgundian, Germanic, and Italianate people who formed the Swiss Confederation found a common cause in rebuffing imperial efforts from all sides: rejecting French, Habsburg, Lombard, and Piedmont overlordship. The Swiss talents for precision machinery from cuckoo clocks to hydropower generators, chemicals from explosives to pharmaceuticals, and culinary delights from fondue to chocolate, all driven by a genius for industrial organization and distribution, continue to bring the country customers from all over the world.

In 1945, after the second "war to end all wars," the Swiss people overwhelmingly rejected membership in the United Nations. Not until a narrow national vote in 2003 did they join the UN. In national polls, Swiss voters also rejected membership in the European Union, rightly fearing EU bureaucratic interference with Swiss privacy and banking laws. In 2004, Switzerland signed several bilateral accords with the EU. A few years ago, a national ballot soundly rejected a specific proposal to ease Swiss bank secrecy laws, and more recent polls support this view. Since 1992, Switzerland has been a member of both the World Bank and the International Monetary Fund.

After each of these national plebiscites, even greater amounts of foreign cash flowed into Swiss banks, confirming the widespread notion that Switzerland is the place to safeguard cash and other personal assets. It is currently estimated that Swiss banks manage at least one third of all assets held offshore by the world's wealthy, an estimated three to four trillion U.S. dollars. As a safe haven for cash, Switzerland has become something of a modern cliché.

Switzerland's bank secrecy law, dating from 1934, has long been under attack from major welfare, high-tax nations, especially Germany and France. In 2009, under great pressure from other nations, Switzerland agreed to adopt tax information exchange standards with 70 tax treaties with other nations.

Switzerland "Once Upon a Time"

The Swiss insurance industry has been about as successful as Swiss banks, especially during the last 30 years of the twentieth century.

In the1980s and early 1990s, you might have read any number of articles about Swiss fixed annuities. They offered the utmost safety, attractive guaranteed returns, the crisis-resistant Swiss franc, and some of the best asset protection in the world. But, as we discussed earlier in Chapter 3 of the book, the IRS changed laws regarding annuities, interest rates were cut, the U.S. dollar found some short-term growth, and the stock market was off to the races.

In short, fixed annuities lost their attraction, and with it went the growing awareness of the Swiss insurance industry.

In the meantime, other things changed. Without a doubt, the Swiss insurance industry is still one of the strongest in the world, and Swiss insurers rank among the best creditors in the world. But Switzerland's conservatism and a number of political developments have led to Swiss life insurance companies paring down their international business, instead using neighboring Liechtenstein as a gateway to international markets.

Additionally, Swiss insurers are following their banking and asset management counterparts and becoming more cautious about doing business with American clients, for fear of far-reaching U.S. regulatory authorities. However, it is still possible to find a few Swiss insurance companies who will work with U.S. investors.

There is another situation to be aware of with regard to how Swiss deferred variable annuities (DVAs) are structured, and it directly impacts American policyholders. Separate, segregated accounts are not possible in Switzerland, and that is the key to obtaining tax deferral according to the IRS. This is why Swiss DVAs are not very attractive to Americans looking to benefit from the legal tax deferral these policies can offer. For citizens from countries other than the United States, Swiss DVAs are still viable.

Many of the Swiss insurers offer more conservative policies, and the customization we discussed in Chapter 4 may not be as easy to find. There has been little innovation in the past 25 years; thus, the range of investment diversification is typically limited to only a handful of investment choices and portfolio options. However, based on the history and success of this powerful country, an equally attractive alternative has sprung up right next door.

Liechtenstein: The Little-Known Nation Offers a Strong Alternative to Switzerland

Tiny Liechtenstein (16 miles long and 3.5 miles wide), not quite as large as the city of Washington, D.C., lies on the east bank of the Rhine River south of Lake Constance between Austria and Switzerland. It consists of low valley land and Alpine peaks. (See Figure 5.2 for a map of Liechtenstein.) The people of Liechtenstein are descended from the Alemanni tribe that migrated into the region sometime after 500 AD. German is still spoken here, although English and other languages are widely used in business.

This monarchy has graced the map of Europe since 1719, but in the last half of the twentieth century, it skillfully promoted itself into a world-class financial center, especially in the areas of banking and insurance. However, a popular travel guide advises somewhat haughtily, "If you nod off, you might miss Liechtenstein all together."

While it has a population of only around 30,000 people, a smaller group of which are actually citizens, this country is home to billions of Swiss francs, U.S. dollars, euros, and just about any other national currency you may wish to keep here. And, much like its tiny appearance on the map, things in this country are low key and very private. They prefer to keep their profile low, but here's where the world's truly wealthy do a lot of business, and with good reason. Liechtenstein has some of the world's strongest banking and financial privacy laws. Plus, it offers world banking and investment direct access through its cooperative neighbor, Switzerland.

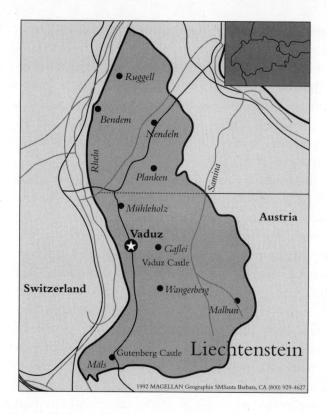

Figure 5.2 Map of Liechtenstein

Source: www.geographicguide.net/europe/maps-europe/maps/liechtenstein-map.gif

History and Overview

The Principality of Liechtenstein was established within the Holy Roman Empire in 1719; it became a sovereign state in 1806. Until the end of World War I, it was closely tied to Austria, but the economic devastation caused by that conflict forced Liechtenstein to enter into a customs and monetary union with Switzerland. Since World War II (in which Liechtenstein remained neutral), the country's low taxes have spurred outstanding economic growth.

With asset protection laws dating as far back as the 1920s; a host of excellent, even unique, legal entities designed for wealth preservation; and strict bank secrecy guaranteed by law, the Principality of Liechtenstein has it all. That strict bank secrecy was relaxed a bit in 2009 but only on an individual case basis and with a showing of probable cause of foreign tax evasion. This policy change occurred after

Liechtenstein came under international pressure, particularly from Germany, to improve transparency in its banking and tax systems.

In the not-so-distant past, one had to be a collector of rare stamps to know that Liechtenstein even existed. In those days, the nation's major export was exquisitely produced postage stamps. In fact, they are still available and highly prized by collectors. Until the 1960s, the principality existed mainly on income from tourism, postage stamp sales, and the export of false teeth.

But in the past 60 years, its lack of taxes, maximum financial privacy, and highly professional financial services propelled Liechtenstein to top rank among the world's wealthiest nations. This historic Rhine Valley country, surrounded by beautiful Alpine peaks, has grown into a major world tax and asset haven, achieving per-capita income levels higher than Germany, France, the United Kingdom, and the United States. This goes to show that countries that offer competitive incentives, such as low taxes and high regulatory standards, usually thrive.

Although only 14 percent of workers are in the financial sector, financial services account for 30 percent of the gross national product. Forty-six percent of the workforce is employed in the industrial sector, while the other 40 percent of employees work in other service activities, such as trade, hotels and restaurants, transport, and public administration. Nearly 12,000 workers commute daily from Austria and Switzerland. Gross domestic product (GDP) has grown as much as 10 percent annually in recent years, and unemployment stays below 2 percent.

The Liechtenstein family of Austria acquired the fiefs of Vaduz and Schellenberg in 1699 and 1713, respectively, and gained the status of an independent principality of the Holy Roman Empire in 1719 under the name Liechtenstein. The French, under Napoleon, occupied the country for a few years, but Liechtenstein regained its independence in 1815 within the new German Confederation. In 1868, after the Confederation dissolved, Liechtenstein disbanded its army of 80 men and declared its permanent neutrality, which was respected during both world wars. In 1919, Liechtenstein entrusted its external relations to neutral Switzerland.

After World War II, Liechtenstein became increasingly important as a financial center, and the country became more prosperous. In 1989, Prince Hans-Adam II succeeded his father to the throne and, in 1996, settled a long-running dispute with Russia over the Liechtenstein family's archives, which had been confiscated during the Soviet occupation of Vienna in 1945 and later moved to Moscow.

Growing as an Important Part of Europe

In 1978, Liechtenstein became a member of the Council of Europe and then joined the UN in 1990, the European Free Trade Association (EFTA) in 1991, and both the European Economic Area (EEA) and World Trade Organization (WTO) in 1995.

Despite its small size and limited natural resources, Liechtenstein has developed into a prosperous, highly industrialized, free-enterprise economy with a vital financial service sector and living standards on par with its large European neighbors. The Liechtenstein economy is widely diversified, with a large number of small businesses.

Low business taxes—the maximum tax rate is 20 percent—and easy incorporation rules have induced many holding or so-called letterbox companies to establish nominal offices in Liechtenstein, providing 30 percent of state revenues. The country participates in a customs union with Switzerland and uses the Swiss franc as its national currency. It imports more than 90 percent of its energy requirements. Liechtenstein has been a member of the EEA (an organization serving as a bridge between EFTA and the EU) since May 1995. The government is working to harmonize its economic policies with those of an integrated Europe.

Liechtenstein: The World's Gateway to International Markets

Joining the EEA in 1995 had a huge impact on Liechtenstein's insurance industry.

Already the "insider's insider," used by world-class Swiss bankers as a gateway for their own business, Liechtenstein's insurance products gained a foothold throughout Europe. Until then, Switzerland and Liechtenstein had a joint insurance industry. Swiss law and supervision applied also to Liechtenstein. But following its induction to the EEA, Liechtenstein created its own insurance law and supervision, and it has done this extremely well.

Liechtenstein basically adapted the best paragraphs from Swiss law and enriched the code by adding others, such as additional benefits found in the laws of countries like Austria. As a result, Liechtenstein insurance law offers unmatched protection and maximum product/investment flexibility (Appendix B-12).

Liechtenstein, much like Luxembourg, has—since its induction into the EEA—evolved from a rank-and-file offshore haven into a "fund center" for Europe as a whole. Legal innovations, not only in the realm of insurance, but also mutual and pension funds, have transformed the country's financial sector and its status abroad. Liechtenstein's bigger brother, Switzerland, now suddenly has a disadvantage compared to Liechtenstein. From Switzerland, it's not possible to cross-border market financial products across the European Union. As a consequence, many of the key Swiss players in the financial sector are establishing a subsidiary in Liechtenstein.

Liechtenstein's direction is clear, and the mentality of the population and their political leaders is highly supportive of these innovations. The country's new direction is also reflected in various laws and in the newly signed Tax Information Exchange Agreement (TIEA) with the U.S. The TIEA is a newly signed information exchange agreement between the United States and Liechtenstein. This agreement (Appendix B-13) regulates the cooperation between the two countries with respect to information exchange also on tax matters. Only specific authorities are allowed to receive and send information, based on specific requests. General "fishing" expeditions are not possible. It is important to understand that this agreement is a positive development for Liechtenstein, on its way to becoming one of Europe's leading financial centers. It makes clear that the Liechtenstein law will protect you if you are an honest investor.

Within the next 5 or 10 years, it is extremely likely that this tiny country will be one of the most successful financial centers in all of Europe.

Concrete Benefits in This Tiny Principality

The policies in Liechtenstein offer strong asset protection from creditors (as we discussed in Chapter 3) as well as investor protection. If a Liechtenstein insurer goes bankrupt, which is completely unprecedented, Article 59a of the Liechtenstein Supervision Act (VersAG) will fully protect you as a policyholder (Appendix B-5). This article explicitly states that the policy's underlying assets are fully segregated from insurer assets in the event of a bankruptcy on the part of the insurer. This should give investors true peace of mind. Thanks to the insurance meltdown in the United States in 2008 and 2009, when companies like AIG tumbled, consumers and potential clients are more aware than ever before that insurance policies are valuable only if the company behind them is rock solid.

Another attractive benefit is the privacy offered under Liechtenstein law. It is a punishable crime for insurance companies or their employees to release client information to a third party unless a crime is involved. This means that if a U.S. litigation lawyer happened to discover that you had a foreign insurance policy and decided to go on a hunting expedition to see what he could find, it would be impossible. Even if the lawyer somehow learned the name of the insurance company and had your policy number, a call to the insurance company would turn up nothing. When it comes to defending yourself from being a target of a lawsuit, especially a frivolous one, the lower your wealth profile and the more difficult it is to assess your true net worth, the better off you are.

But perhaps one of the tiny country's greatest strengths is the incredible access it has to the world markets.

Liechtenstein insurance companies have the right to open separate, segregated custodian accounts for the underlying assets of insurance policies with basically every bank within Europe and Switzerland, and it may employ any asset manager in the world to manage those assets. This is really a world-class opportunity to diversify your wealth well beyond the U.S. borders! Liechtenstein law also permits that the policyholder may self-direct the underlying account. However, as we discussed at length in Chapter 4, countries like the United States will not allow a policy to grow tax privileged if you self-direct the investments.

Liechtenstein insurance policies will also allow you to adjust life coverage on a specific insurance or annuity contract. A policy may include no life coverage, or the insured may apply for additional coverage—it all depends on the wishes of the policyholder. In some cases, certain countries such as the United States will require a certain amount of life coverage in order for the policy to grow tax deferred.

Liechtenstein has embraced its role as a leader and innovator in the insurance market. As such, many new policies and variations of traditional policies are being developed to meet the ever-changing needs of a twenty-first-century investor.

Isle of Man: Freedom to Flourish and the Creativity to Make It Happen

The windswept island with its strong national pride and centuries of history is a unique financial center. (For a map of the Isle of Man, see Figure 5.3.) Part of the Norwegian Kingdom of the Hebrides until the thirteenth century, when it was ceded to Scotland, the Isle of Man came under the British crown in 1765. Current concerns include reviving the almost extinct Manx Gaelic language. The Isle of Man is a British crown dependency but is not part of the United Kingdom or the European Union. However, the U.K. Government remains constitutionally responsible for its defense and international representation.

Offshore banking, manufacturing, and tourism are key sectors of the economy.

Figure 5.3 Map of the Isle of Man

Source: http://powayusd.sdcoe.k12.ca.us/teachers/dsykes/im-map.gif.

The financial sector is the largest single sector, employing more than 20 percent of the total workforce of nearly 40,000. More than 40 licensed banks (including many international banks) offer comprehensive, discreet, and confidential services that compare favorably with the banks in Switzerland or Liechtenstein.

The government offers incentives to high-technology companies (like the CVI company that made the laser optics with which NASA's Phoenix Lander spotted snow on Mars in 2008) and financial institutions to locate on the island. This has paid off in expanding employment opportunities in high-income industries. As a result, agriculture and fishing, once the mainstays of the economy, have declined in their contributions to GDP. The Isle of Man also attracts online gambling sites and the film industry. Trade is mostly with the United Kingdom. The Isle of Man enjoys free access to EU markets.

Tynwald and Freedom to Flourish

The Isle of Man's 1,030-year-old Tynwald, which is the world's oldest parliament, is thought to have been the first to give women the vote.

That innovative spirit lives on.

Currently, the Isle of Man government[1] runs what will soon be the biggest offshore register for corporate and private jets, and another for super-yachts, which generates hundreds of jobs for lawyers, insurers, and tax experts.

In 1995, the government decided to develop a film industry. It offered to pay 25 percent of production costs in return for a share of the profits. In the 14 years since, 91 films have been made on the island, and the government has earned £3 for every £1 invested. Islanders talk nonchalantly of seeing Renée Zellweger jogging along the beach or Johnny Depp in a pub.

"Freedom to flourish" is the island's marketing slogan, but it's more than a slogan—it's actually their way of life. Aside from handsome tax breaks, it offers entrepreneurs friendly legislation, ready finance, a nimble bureaucracy, and easy access to politicians; their numbers are in the telephone book, and Tony Brown, the chief minister, works in his electrician's shop on Saturday mornings.

It is an approach that has reaped rewards in recent years.

In spite of grumbling from London about its tax haven status, the island has enjoyed 26 consecutive years of growth. It has no national debt, an unemployment rate of just 2.2 percent, and has avoided the global recession. Per-capita income, 24 percent lower than Britain's in 1996, is 18 percent higher now, at about $35,000.

"It's the greatest economic success story nobody has ever heard of," says Chris Corlett, head of the Department of Trade and Industry. The island does not flaunt its newfound wealth, but it is apparent from the Mercedes, Porsches, Morgans, and Bentleys and from the conversion of dilapidated hotels into fine sea front apartments.

Even old-timers agree that life is better:[2] the young no longer have to leave to find work, the government pays for islanders to have medical treatment or university educations in Britain, and it is planning to give every schoolchild a free laptop.

Despite this ravenous taste for innovation, however, offshore annuities and VULs from the Isle of Man do have a few sizeable hurdles you won't find in Switzerland or Liechtenstein.

Some Obstacles for Annuities and Other Policies

First, the Isle isn't a part of the European Union due to its status for the past few years as an offshore haven for the EEA. Thus, to some degree, the Isle of Man is politically isolated. Without membership in the biggest economic unions, it is sometime challenging for the island to work with the larger reinsurance companies based in Europe and the United Kingdom. Also, their status as an offshore center means that, at times, some of its products aren't as widely accepted throughout the world.

Additionally, the Isle is a crown dependency.

This introduces the fiscal weakness of the United Kingdom into the equation, which could make some people uncomfortable. For example, Gordon Brown decided in 2009 to slash the budgets of crown dependencies by upwards of 24 percent, leading to an immediate, unprecedented fiscal crisis for the Isle and other dependencies. Concerns sprang up about the Isle's credit rating, and such a large-scale event could have a major impact on your business with the jurisdiction.

Make no mistake that compared to Switzerland and Liechtenstein, this tiny jurisdiction follows close behind. It checks all the boxes. It is a world leader in democratic stability; it has a 1,000-year tradition of respecting property and privacy, and the country's unique spirit of innovation will surely carry it into a brighter future.

But due to the factors mentioned immediately above, we can't recommend the Isle of Man *as strongly* as some others.

Luxembourg: In the Heart of Europe, a Thriving Financial Center Was Born

Luxembourg is located in western Europe, between France and Germany. (See Figure 5.4 for a map of Luxembourg.) Founded in 963, the country shares borders with Germany to the east, Belgium to the west, and France to the south. Luxembourg is also a part of the Benelux group, along with Belgium and the Netherlands. Since 1922, Luxembourg has had a fully integrated monetary and economic union with its larger neighbor, Belgium.

After 400 years of domination by various European nations, Luxembourg was granted the status of grand duchy by the Congress of Vienna on June 9, 1815. Although locals consider 1835 (Treaty of London) to be its year of independence, it was not granted political autonomy

Figure 5.4 Map of Luxembourg

Source: www.faqs.org/docs/factbook/maps/lu-map.gif.

until 1839 under King William I of the Netherlands, who also was the grand duke of Luxembourg. In 1867, Luxembourg was recognized as fully independent and guaranteed perpetual neutrality, but it lost more than half of its territory to Belgium in 1839.

Overrun by Germany in both world wars, it ended its neutrality in 1948, when it entered into the Benelux Customs Union and became a charter member of the North Atlantic Treaty Organization (NATO) in 1949. It is also one of the six original members of the European Union. In 1957, Luxembourg became one of the six founding countries of the European Economic Community (later to become the European Union) and joined the euro currency area.

Banking and Business Haven

Although the nation's international banking activity dates back to the late nineteenth century, Luxembourg did not hit its stride as a financial center until about 25 years ago. This process developed from forces over which Luxembourg had no control. There were multiple developments.

First, there was a growth of foreign investment in selected European Common Market nations during the mid-1960s. Then there was the U.S. imposition of an interest equalization tax in the 1980s that drove American corporations to borrow abroad. There were German capital flow restrictions and mandatory lending ratios. Then the Swiss introduced a 35 percent Swiss withholding tax on bank accounts and other interests. There were currency exchange controls in France and, finally, stiff bank account reporting rules in nearby Holland.

To avoid these circumstances, astute western Europeans and Americans began searching for a safe place to invest their money. They also needed a convenient place to conduct global business with maximum freedom and lower taxes. Centrally located in the middle of Europe, Luxembourg and its banks offer a perfect solution.

About 60 percent of all Luxembourg bank activity is now denominated in euros. Another one third is in U.S. dollars. Roughly 21,000 people are employed directly or indirectly in the Duchy's more than 150 banks, and nearly 16 percent of the GDP flows from banking business. German banks, in particular, operate here to escape domestic withholding taxes on interest and dividend loan limitations on corporate customers, and they account for over 50 percent of all banking business. They also use the nation to deal in gold, as Luxembourg imposes no value-added tax (VAT).

Although Luxembourg, like all EU members, suffered from the global economic slump in the early part of this decade, the country continues to enjoy an extraordinarily high standard of living—GDP per capita ranks third in the world, after Liechtenstein and Qatar. After two years of strong economic growth in 2006–2007, turmoil in the world financial markets slowed Luxembourg's economy in 2008, but growth remained above the European average and remained so in 2009.

Much like Liechtenstein, Luxembourg had a fairly strict bank secrecy law that was made less strict in 2009. This policy change occurred after the grand duchy came under international pressure from the G-20 nations to improve transparency in its banking and tax systems.

Luxembourg insurance policies do allow for separate segregated accounts so when properly structured, they are able to comply with the IRS tax deferral regulations. In addition, the separate, segregated account provides you with a good level of investor protection should the insurer go bankrupt. However, their policies are not as flexible as the ones offered by Liechtenstein with respect to your choice of custodian banks as well as the underlying investments. If asset protection is an important factor to you, be aware that Luxembourg policies do not offer any such coverage.

LEVEL II JURISDICTIONS: NOT AS STRONG, EQUALLY STABLE—SECONDARY CANDIDATES

Beyond the handful of top-flight financial havens described so far, there are a few more alternatives you may wish to consider.

Again, we'll emphasize the fact that these jurisdictions fall a little short in one area or another. As a general statement, they lack the centuries-long traditions you'll find in our top selections. And while that may seem like a pretty intangible measurement, it can make all the difference when you're looking for peace of mind.

But that's not to disparage them.

Out of the remaining 250 or so countries in the world, these four jurisdictions still come out ahead of the pack. They're mostly world-renowned financial havens, and while their insurance industries may not be as developed and well known for their annuity business, they can still provide a great home for other offshore structures like trusts, captive insurance, and offshore bank accounts. The fact that most of these havens resemble a tropical paradise . . . well, let's say that didn't hurt their standings either.

Since you may at some point at least consider doing business with one of these jurisdictions, let's take a moment to briefly discuss the strengths of each one. We will focus on their history and a little on current news and a few of their signature financial service offerings so that you're ready to make an informed decision when the time comes.

The Republic of Ireland

It's not a Caribbean paradise, and for most people it's not even the kind of country they'd consider a financial haven. But skip over Ireland at your own risk.

During the 1990s, Ireland became known as the "Celtic Tiger" because of a sharp economic upturn that resembled the tiger economies of Asia. At the same time, the Irish government instituted a number of incentives for investment and introduced a low rate of corporation tax (12.5 percent contrasted with 39.5 percent in the United States). Government-backed investment incentives; a low rate of corporation tax; and a highly educated, young, flexible workforce all combined to make Ireland the desired location for over 1,100 overseas companies to base their European operations.

Unlike many of the socialist welfare states of Europe, years ago Ireland chose the corporate low-tax route, and as a result has become the prosperity powerhouse of Europe. As a result, almost half a million new jobs were created in Ireland, a phenomenon that changed the outlook of its people and the profile of its society and economy radically, and for the better.

Businesses and workers from all over Europe flocked to Ireland as new jobs expanded under business taxes ranging from 10 percent to a maximum of 25 percent, with a standard rate of 12.5 percent for most. And with this recent surge in business, Ireland's offerings to foreign investors and savers have increased dramatically both in quantity and potential.

Most recently, Ireland has been suffering from the soft global economy. Plus, it is feeling the pain of its own real estate market crash due to a rapid appreciation in home prices in the early 2000s coupled with historically low interest rates. Yet, Ireland still has a growing insurance market that offers flexible policies and separate, segregated accounts, so investors are protected in event of the insurer's bankruptcy. However, Ireland does not have any privacy or asset protection laws to shield investors.

The Cayman Islands

Just hearing the word *offshore* makes many Americans think of the Cayman Islands. Everyone from Goldman Sachs to former U.S. presidents have used this classy, nearby financial center to establish access to global markets and other financial products.

Located in the Caribbean, the three-island group (Grand Cayman, Cayman Brac, and Little Cayman) is south of Cuba and northwest of Jamaica.

With no direct taxation, the islands are a thriving financial center. Many thousands of offshore companies are registered here, including hundreds of banks and trust companies. Banking assets exceed US$500 billion. Ultimately, the financial industry here is under indirect control of the British government in London, and the Labour Party has forced changes relaxing financial privacy and exchange of tax information. The islands now have in place a Tax Information Exchange Treaty with the United States and an increasing number of other nations, including the United Kingdom.

Tourism is another mainstay, accounting for about 70 percent of GDP and 75 percent of foreign currency earnings. The tourist industry is aimed at the luxury market and caters mainly to visitors from North America. Total tourist arrivals exceeded 1.2 million in 2000, with 600,000 from the United States. About 90 percent of the islands' food and consumer goods must be imported. Caymanians enjoy one of the highest outputs per capita and one of the highest standards of living in the world.

But despite its proximity and its tourist appeal, the main reason why the Caymans became a world-class financial center was its strict privacy—and not just privacy, but near absolute secrecy. Guaranteed by law and enforced by local courts, foreigners were shielded from scrutiny. Even in the case of criminal proceedings, a lengthy judicial process was needed to pierce this wall of secrecy.

But that was the old Caymans, before their colonial masters in London and their largest neighbor, the United States, forced them to compromise on their bank and financial secrecy. Today, Cayman policies do offer the necessary segregated accounts; however, there is no asset protection or privacy laws to shield investors. If this had still been the case, the Caymans could have very well met our criteria for a top ranking, as they once had the best tradition of financial privacy in the whole hemisphere.

Singapore

While the Caymans of the 1980s gave American investors an unfettered gateway to the world, Singapore has come to occupy a very similar position for Asian investors and even their Western counterparts.

Singapore has an open economy, with strong service and manufacturing sectors as well as excellent international trading links. The government's strategy includes cutting costs, increasing productivity, improving infrastructure, and encouraging higher-value–added industries. In applied technology, per-capita output, investment, and labor discipline, Singapore has the key attributes of a developed country.

Singapore is actively recruiting wealthy businessmen as residents. For those active in offshore finance, this is a match made in financial heaven because the island city-state is seeking to establish itself as Asia's newest private banking hub by luring the super-wealthy away from places such as Hong Kong and Switzerland.

Singapore's strengthened bank secrecy laws are one thing that makes this country attractive; the government's allowing foreigners, especially Europeans, who meet its wealth requirements, to buy land and become permanent residents is another. The goal is to attract private wealth from across the globe.

Many Swiss banks are beefing up their operations in Singapore to capitalize on the new business opportunities. The number of private banks operating in Singapore has nearly doubled, to 35, in the past six years, officials say. Authorities estimate that money managed by private banks in Singapore has grown 20 percent each year since 2000, to more than US$200 billion today.

In terms of financial services, particularly its trust business and the legal backing thereof, Singapore is easily on par with some of the best in the world, including Panama and Bermuda. And if the next decade or so unfolds as expected, Singapore could soon be counted among the best financial centers in the entire world. But not just yet. . . .

While the insurance companies offer segregated accounts, and the country has tax exchange agreements with all the major nations, we still have some concern about the political situation.

When Singapore gained independence from Great Britain in 1965, the country moved to an autocratic leader, Lee Kuan Yew. In 1990, Yew's son replaced him in his official capacities. This one-party state does not tolerate dissent or opposition, and some of the severe laws that keep crime to a minimum also limit freedoms. While this enforced stability has been attractive to many outside investors and has resulted in massive foreign investment in the country, we are still a bit cautious. Should the regime wish to make changes to any current policies, it could do so virtually overnight with no discussion.

Nevis

If you're not in the business of working with offshore financial centers, then there's a good chance you've never even heard of Nevis. But if there's one haven country that has all the things needed for smooth offshore financial operations, it's the two-island federation of St. Kitts and Nevis.

Its pro-offshore laws have existed for over two decades, so there is plenty of experience and precedent in the local courts, and the legislative assembly keeps the applicable laws current. There are well-established offshore financial service companies that can do what you want, and some have convenient U.S. branch offices.

The country as a whole owes much to its success as the business-friendly "Delaware of the Caribbean." Over the last two decades, its parliament has adopted and constantly updated excellent offshore corporation, trust, and limited liability company laws, augmented by strict financial privacy.

Nevis is simply taking advantage of the worldwide growth in medical, legal, and professional malpractice lawsuits. Legislative and judicial imposition of no-fault personal liability on corporate officers and directors has become a nasty fact of business life. A Nevis trust places personal assets beyond the reach of foreign governments, litigious plaintiffs, creditors, and contingency fee lawyers.

This small, two-island country's greatest assets are its considerable natural beauty and Nevis as a financial center. To exploit potential tourism, the government has agreements with foreign-owned hotel and condominium developments. St. Kitts is a popular tourist destination, with white sand beaches, deep sea fishing, golf, tennis, and casino gambling. Since 1994, the federation has been part of the Association of Caribbean States (ACS) trading bloc of over 60 million people.

The Nevis insurance policies do offer segregated accounts; however, it is a very small country that is dependent on tourism and friendly relations with its neighbors. Its largest neighbor is the United States, and it is possible that the United States could exert pressure on this tiny nation if any of its current financial regulations fell out of favor. That's a potential risk to all who do business here.

Bermuda

A self-governing British overseas territory, Bermuda is a major international financial center. In the early days, their focus was based largely on reinsurance companies. But they have expanded, and now about 30 percent of the world's captive self-insurance companies are domiciled here. The insurance industry is very substantial—active companies have approximately $172 billion in assets and write almost $50 billion in annual gross premiums.

The sophistication of the insurance industry in Bermuda is not the only appeal, as this jurisdiction also offers client protection laws, which are important. Under the Bermuda Private Act, insurance policies and their underlying assets cannot be seized by a creditor of the policyholder or the beneficiary, except in certain situations, which are defined in the Bermuda law. Also, protection from frivolous lawsuits is possible, especially when you consider that the mere threat of litigation in Bermuda can be an expensive exercise.

It is possible to use a separate account with insurance companies in Bermuda to ensure that assets are segregated from the assets of the insurance company. Also, as we discussed earlier in the book, traditional insurance policies have long been a part of global financial planning, much like trusts. Some Bermuda insurance companies can write a policy that can provide trustlike benefits without the drafting, custodian, trustee, ongoing legal, regulatory, or reporting requirements typically associated with a trust. While this shows the progressive and creative nature of the insurance companies located in Bermuda, as countries such as the United States and the United Kingdom attempt to extend their political and legal wishes extraterritorially, our concern is that some of the strengths offered by this country will continue to diminish.

Since Bermuda is still colony of the United Kingdom and a neighbor of the United States, it has been forced to take orders from London with regard to its privacy laws. Also, the island has had to succumb to political pressure from the United States regarding not only financial privacy but also over tax reporting issues by U.S. citizens. While we welcome the financial housecleaning and some of the stricter laws, we are concerned that Bermuda is very U.S. focused. There are many North American insurance carriers based here, and that gives the United States a large presence.

Bermuda's proximity to the United States and its previous actions toward American-based desires, coupled with the influence from the politic decisions in London, is why we have chosen to list Bermuda as a Level II jurisdiction, rather than a first-tier location.

LEVEL III JURISDICTIONS: UP-AND-COMING HAVENS AND THOSE WITH FLAWS

Jurisdiction is a key consideration when you are looking for a domicile for a private placement policy. As you can see, we have categorized our list into three sections.

The countries listed in Level III are relatively new to the world of international insurance or have political situations that we believe introduce additional risk. We will touch on Brunei, the Seychelles, and the Bahamas only briefly, as we do not consider these appropriate jurisdictions at this time. Yet, we feel it's important to share our reasoning so that you can make an informed decision when considering your personal situation.

Brunei—The Tiny Jewel of Southeast Asia

Brunei is a dot on the map with a geographic area about the size of the state of Delaware. It is located near Malaysia in Southeast Asia. The country has been ruled by the same family for over six centuries. Brunei benefits from extensive petroleum and natural gas fields, the source of one of the highest per-capita GDPs in Asia. The sultan is one of the wealthiest men on earth.

The country gained complete independence from Britain in 1984, and in the past several years a small financial industry has started to develop, yet there is certainly no financial tradition in this country. However, more recently, Brunei has come up with some interesting insurance laws very similar to the Liechtenstein protection laws.

Insurers are regulated under the International Insurance and Takaful Order, 2002, with the assets protected in the event of bankruptcy of the insurance company. There is also now a provision for asset protection. Under the Brunei Insurance and Takaful Order, the assets are protected in the event of your own bankruptcy, so the beneficiaries are entitled to the life insurance policy.

Plus, under Brunei legislation, international investors are protected and an insurance policy is subject to complete confidentiality. As you can see, they are taking a page from the most attractive aspects of Liechtenstein law.

However, an investor should think carefully before choosing this jurisdiction. Brunei is an absolute monarchy, whereby the sultan of Brunei is both head of state and head of government. In nondemocratic countries the laws can change very quickly, and what was an advantage for you today may turn out to be a disadvantage for tomorrow.

Seychelles—Up and Coming

The Seychelles is a beautiful island nation off the east coast of Africa, just north of Madagascar. Most of us probably know the Seychelles as a great travel destination for diving and white beaches, rather than for banking and finance.

However, the Seychelles has recently introduced a number of laws in order to position itself as an international financial center. In fact, establishing a company structure in the Seychelles is become more popular, especially for Indian citizens, who are neighbors to the islands. In 2008, the Seychelles introduced a new insurance act as well as a mutual fund act and hedge fund act.

The Insurance Act contains provisions for the licensing of offshore insurance companies, insurance managers, and principal insurance representatives. Besides domestic insurance, the act also regulates non-domestic insurance business in an attractive way. The act contains a section for client protection, and the law provides for full confidentiality, except in cases involving criminal investigation.

In addition, according to section 17 of the Insurance Act, there is investor protection in the event of bankruptcy so that the policy assets are segregated from the assets of the insurer. This is another very attractive benefit, and it leads us to believe that this country could play a future role in the international insurance market.

However, it goes without saying that this country currently lacks proven financial experience and track record. For international insurance, it is still too young; however, it should be watched carefully. After their laws have been put to a few tests and passed them well, the Seychelles could become a very robust jurisdiction.

The Bahamas—Changes Make it Unattractive

During the twentieth century, the Bahamas, a chain of islands located off the southeast corner of the United States, bloomed into a major tax and asset protection haven, especially for nearby Americans. It offered tax exemptions for foreigners and a series of very well crafted laws allowing trusts, offshore banks, business corporations, and insurance products—all wrapped in maximum financial privacy protected by law.

Because so many Americans used the Bahamas as their favorite offshore haven, the islands came under heavy pressure from the U.S. government and the IRS because of suspected tax evasion. Then there was a second issue—drug smuggling and money laundering. Starting in 2000, the then-Bahamian government adopted a series of U.S.-demanded laws to clean up any problems in its financial sector; however, that seriously diminished the country's role as an offshore haven.

While this jurisdiction had developed a strong international insurance base, most insurance carriers still doing business in the Bahamas are U.S. based, so there is little jurisdictional protection for an investor. Unfortunately, we feel financial independence of the Bahamas has been compromised, and any benefits it may have offered are no longer valid. It's best to look elsewhere.

THE SECOND PART OF THE EQUATION: SELECTING THE RIGHT COMPANY

Finding the right jurisdiction is the first part of the equation. Next, you have to find the right company for your policy as well.

Ideally, the best insurance companies will have a long, stable track record. They'll show a solid financial basis and a history of responsible management you can count on to do the job without getting too creative or greedy.

Your ideal company will also be one that doesn't have any subsidiaries in your home country. That will ensure that the company can act independently, without unnecessary pressure from outside influences. If your chosen company has *any* operations in the 50 states, then American lawyers will have a much easier time arguing jurisdiction over your assets, and that's something we're going to great lengths to rid ourselves of in the first place.

Additionally, the mentality of management should be generally conservative, yet it should be open-minded toward marginal innovations and flexible products and solutions without getting *too* creative or too greedy.

Furthermore, you want your insurer to be independent from banks and asset managers in order to avoid any conflict of interest. A company like AIG, for example, would be the last possible place you'd want to have a policy. Stuck in between government shareholders, Wall Street counterparties, and main street policyholders, you're virtually guaranteed not to benefit from the best managers and conditions available to you.

It is also important to understand that vetting a foreign insurance company is not as simple as looking for the "AAA" stamped on the front door. People are often surprised to hear that most insurance companies in Switzerland and Liechtenstein don't even have a rating. But why be shocked? When strictly enforced regulations create an industry where a sub-AAA rating (by Western standards) would be illegal, what is the point of the letter grade?

In our opinion, throughout most Western economies, the ratings are made by commercially driven companies. If your company wants an AAA rating, you pay for it. And if ratings agencies want your repeat business, they give you a good rating. It's as simple as that. Keep in mind that Lehman Brothers was a good repeat customer—until they went bankrupt, that is. And it wasn't until six hours *after* Lehman declared bankruptcy that their rating was finally downgraded.

How to Know Where to Start

Finally, realize that this might not be a very easy task and that often it makes sense to work with an adviser who has access to multiple international insurance companies and can work with you and your family to find the best fit for your needs. In order to make the most of your conversation with an adviser, we recommend that you do your homework in advance so that you are prepared. The following list of questions will help you start thinking about all the pieces that an adviser will need to consider to create the right wealth-saving solution for you:

- What are your liquidity needs for the remainder of your life?
- What types of threats concern you and how much asset protection do you need?
- What is your current tax situation? Will this change in the future? Will you have a large estate tax bill, or can you reduce it?
- What are your investment goals? What is your risk tolerance? How risk averse are you? What is your investment time frame? Ten years or 50?
- How do you want your estate to pass to your heirs? Do you have a clear plan for the transition of those assets?

Once you have invested time in defining your goals, you are ready to work with a professional to find the right solution and the best jurisdiction for that solution.

CHAPTER 6

HEADING OUT INTO THE UNKNOWN WITH CONFIDENCE

In conclusion, we hope this book has helped open your eyes a little bit.

Not just to the threats you face as a twenty-first-century saver and investor—as many as there are—but also to the opportunities as well, the unconsidered possibilities of a world with unparalleled access and communication. Because it's only when you pull back and *really* consider the long term, as we have in these pages, that you can make the most informed decision. And we believe that it is possible to insure your future.

It's true that, historically speaking, the United States seems to be heading the way of so many other empires.

America's rise to global superiority began in a time much like today, when another empire overstretched its bounds and the financial world imploded. Against the backdrop of funny-money loans and financial witchcraft, America stood alone—a bastion of free enterprise, where each person had the right to conduct his business unobstructed and unharassed. Americans worked hard for low wages, they saved diligently, and they endured hardship to build tremendous wealth within their country.

But then, as we know all too well, it gradually took a turn for the worse.

Hard work, true grit, and determination carried America as far and as fast as it could go, but like so many other nations before us, we demanded more. And we got it in the form of paper money, deficit spending, and revolutionary new entitlement programs. Hard times during the Depression confounded a generation that had known only progress and plenty, and from that the New Deal was born. It reshaped the way Americans looked at their government, what they expected from it. That shift would be carried only further in the cultural and civil rights revolutions of the 1960s, when it became clear that the laws of the government were no longer expected to *follow* the populace but to *lead* it.

America changed rapidly in that time—and it would seem to be for the better.

Unfortunately, few of those changes furthered the bailiwick of American success and wealth building, the preservation of free enterprise. Instead, many had the opposite effect, making it less attractive to run a business by stifling industrial growth, and raising the cost (and risk) of ownership. It's becoming harder and harder to get wealthy and stay wealthy in America. And at a time when so many of the world's promising emerging markets are breaking down unnecessary regulations and socialized industries, America is doing the opposite.

Now, soon to be crushed under the weight of its own debts and obligations as our nation reaches the peak of its prime, we've exposed the many potential disasters that could unfurl in the coming years and decades. We've discussed how a lifetime of "borrow-and-spend" politicians has traded away the value of the U.S. dollar. We've also talked about Social Security and Fannie Mae and Freddie Mac, a host of short-term solutions that were never scuttled or properly overhauled, left to fester on the nation's balance sheet until they created a problems of exponential proportions.

The most concerning aspect is that it is becoming clear that the spending and entitlements have already had a grave impact on our American psyche.

It's effectively deferred social unrest. It's helped people like you and us to overlook the glaring problems with America's economy—and with our government. Cheap mortgages and social insurance will likely be seen in the eyes of history as America's version of "bread and circuses," and little more. This was something to tide the people over while our economy disappeared out from under us.

To be fair, this wasn't the only distraction. We were also distracted by a new kind of threat.

Identity theft, frivolous lawsuits, divorce settlements—Americans of the twenty-first century face a lifetime of complicated situations and potentially disastrous run-ins with the law—or outlaws. And when it comes to your money, it doesn't really matter which side these threats are on—it will cost you either way.

Our aim has been to make you aware of all those threats so you could prepare for them on your own terms, not to have you lie awake at night.

So we gave you an easy-to-remember list of what you're going to need to thrive in the financial world of the twenty-first century:

- You need protection from a rapidly growing government that will change the U.S. economy and marketplace, which entails a *new* kind of diversification.
- You need protection from the continuing erosion of the value of the U.S. dollar thanks to federal spending and government stealth.
- You need protection from frivolous lawsuits, which will continue to explode as those with deep pockets are sought out as targets.
- And all this saving and investing is a smart move only if your ultimate goal is to be able to benefit from it in the future or make sure that the people you care about benefit after you're gone. So proper estate planning is a must.

With those needs in mind, we set out to find the best opportunities available, quickly learning that the biggest obstacle was just getting *access* to those opportunities.

At first you might have thought your 401(k) or pension plan would do the trick.

After all, it offers tax deferral and reasonable access to world markets—isn't that close enough?

Not quite, as you read in Chapter 2.

While a U.S.-based retirement plan will offer *some* access to global market funds, exchange-traded funds, and foreign companies trading on American exchanges, it won't give you the pinpoint access you'll need to really crank up your returns. And while you won't be able to self-direct your offshore variable annuity, you *will* be able to place it in the capable hands of one of the world's top asset managers.

So, for example, you could outline a strategy that targets the most promising up-and-coming investments in a specific emerging market. After all, as we showed you, many of these countries are currently building industry and infrastructure for the twentieth century, let alone the twenty-first. Traditionally safe investments like utilities, food companies, and drug producers can offer performance to best anything you've seen in domestic markets over the past decade.

While American exchanges were busy treading water for the first decade of the new century, foreign bourses soared upwards of 1,000 percent or more. The change is apparent. The world's emerging markets are packed with billions who have never known wealth, who are finally able to save and invest, and who appreciate the value of a day's hard work. And—perhaps the most startling statistic of all—most of them are still children, with the average age in many emerging markets below 30 years.

So the fierce competition, the saving, spending, and investment we've seen up to this point may very well be just the tip of the iceberg.

This is a trend that simply can't be ignored. Because while the world's emerging markets begin to dominate global growth, America's economy will only flounder more. Spending and entitlement will have to expand and make up for the lost opportunities (the 2009 stimulus was just the first taste), debt will continue to balloon, and our nation's creditors will gradually realize the next generation won't be able to return the value they've invested.

That's the point where domestic retirement savings, like the self-directed IRA mentioned earlier, start to look particularly vulnerable.

But, worst of all, it's not just your pension plan or retirement account, because in this wonderful world of finance, literally everything is interconnected. So the government doesn't have to go after your savings directly. After all, who needs your dollars when they've got a printing press in the basement? And that printing press has been awfully busy in recent years. We might not feel the consequences today or tomorrow, but at some point, the inevitable *will* catch up with American savers.

Now standing on its last leg as the world reserve currency, the dollar's power is being chipped away at as it's replaced in foreign vaults from Russia to Iran and India in favor of gold or the euro. At this point, no one can tell you whether it will come in the form of some panicked crash or in a gradual, mellow decline, but one thing is certain: the American dollar is no longer the global titan it once was. It's an asset that ever-fewer foreigners really want to own, and that's going to affect the way your savings spend decades down the road.

The foreign private placement policy is a great alternative to diversifying yourself and storing your savings in a number of different currencies, rather than just in dollars. And when you step back to consider all the possibilities, there is one benefit that stands out in stark contrast against the field of conventional alternatives—namely, asset protection.

Asset protection can be a hard thing to define, since the threats it protects against come in so many different forms. Almost all of these threats are characteristically unexpected, and unless you're already in a field that routinely acknowledges these threats, like the medical field with malpractice insurance, they can go unnoticed.

With an offshore insurance policy, you get the pick of the litter.

You can enter a policy with an insurer in a country like Liechtenstein—one of our top recommended jurisdictions—where asset protection is guaranteed by law. They won't protect a criminal, and they won't protect a hastily constructed policy created in the face of imminent bankruptcy. That is exactly why you can expect a high degree of safety that is unparalleled worldwide. And that's just the *legal* aspect of it.

Remember that moving your money to a country like Liechtenstein creates a major *psychological* barrier as well. A significantly higher cost barrier and the specter of highly defensive courts will keep the less scrupulous from even considering the prospect of harassing you. As the years wear on, we expect this to be one of the most significant, though understated, benefits of the offshore variable annuity.

But it's not the most understated benefit of these foreign policies.

That crown most certainly goes to the estate planning possibilities—something that few of us devote enough time to considering. In addition to acting like your own personalized retirement account, the private placement policy can be structured as a life insurance contract. But distributions to beneficiaries can be made much more tailored than those from American insurance policies. In fact, the payments can almost be structured like those from a trust. So the same flexibility you get in terms of investment and structure can be expected when it is time to distribute your estate.

The private placement policy can continue paying out and switch to your heirs, it can pay a lump sum to family or charity—add that to whatever kind of customization you need to fit your personal situation, and you'll find an estate planning solution that renders the alternatives irrelevant.

AN UNCOMMON SOLUTION ON THE ROAD LESS TRAVELED

If you've had a little trouble wrapping your head around the whole concept of an offshore variable annuity throughout the course of this book, we don't blame you. We've all been there.

One of the annuity's biggest strengths is its flexibility. As a result, it can be hard to form a concrete idea of what defines a variable annuity. What *defines* it is that it is geared to pay out a stream of income based on the variable returns of the underlying portfolio. But beyond that simple specification, each one is different, like snowflakes. That's because they're tailor-made to fit the individual and the situation you find them in.

For one individual, it means peace of mind in knowing his daughters will be comfortably taken care of long after he's gone. For another, it's a promise he made to his family and his favorite nonprofit organizations. For yet another, it's the best alternative when life insurers have shunned his business despite his immense wealth.

We've seen these solutions take a number of forms in so many places. Yet they got their start here, in the America of the 1930s, 1940s, and 1950s, as teachers and civil servants needed an alternative to the traditional retirement account, one that could offer the boost of tax-deferred growth and help bridge their meager income into retirement. Out of those needs some of the first commercial policies were offered.

Likewise, in the high-flying investment age of the 1980s, advisers and asset managers took a new look at these policies. With interest rates falling rapidly, ultra-safe government bonds were a "no-brainer" investment for many of their clients. Annuities offered the client a vehicle that guaranteed lifetime income.

And when savvy investors began to look across the ocean for protection for the U.S. dollar, the Swiss fixed annuity became a widely utilized solution.

Today, the saver and investor of the twenty-first century faces a situation that's more complicated than ever. And after all these pages and charts and statistics, we feel comfortable in saying that you, dear reader, appreciate not only the situation you face, but the potential of the solutions within arm's reach.

With the power of a private placement policy, you can leverage the access of the world's most celebrated and widely used financial hubs to plug your money into any opportunity almost anywhere in the world. You can put the world's most successful investors and hedge fund managers in charge of your savings and rest assured that while you sip your coffee in Topeka, Kansas, your savings are hard at work in Mumbai or Beijing, in Rio or Johannesburg, where you'll find the kind of profits best suited to your personal tastes and perspective.

Shortly after you sign your policy, you'll be instantly diversified into the countries and currencies of your choosing. By instructing your insurer for the funds to be invested in foreign stocks, bonds, and currencies, you'll no longer have to worry about "the sinking dollar" or the Treasury bubble. In fact, if you favor a defensive, all-weather strategy, you can take almost all currency risk off the table and invest throughout the world without having to worry about the bucking and crashing of currencies over the years—the value of your savings *will* be protected.

With the simple act of moving your money offshore, you'll ward off potentially dozens of lawsuits from parties not out to actually *win* their suits, but to harass endlessly. And if you choose the right home jurisdiction, you can be certain that your wealth is protected by the rule of law.

On top of all these things, your policy will act as a simple but effective estate planning tool. Along with determining when you'll take your payouts and where you'd like the money invested, you'll select a beneficiary to receive the funds once you're gone. No need for a complex will and testament or $10,000 retainers for estate planning attorneys.

If one thing has remained constant throughout all of our experiences and case studies, it's that the private placement policy is *just a structure*, a means of playing by the rules and to the best of your ability. With the help of capable professionals, you'll be able to satisfy the IRS while still enjoying tax deferral exploring opportunities that are far from the beaten path.

OUR TOP THREE PICKS

Under the umbrella of foreign private placement policies, there are dozens of options. However, there are three types of policies that we believe offer the best potential solution. The first and most widely used is the deferred variable annuity (DVA).

Since the greatest strength of offshore policies in general is flexibility, the DVA makes the absolute most of that flexibility. It should come as no surprise that at the end of all of the research, this often is the most common solution for a large majority of investors. The industry is dominated by these types of policies, with variable universal life (VUL) and frozen cash value (FCV) policies comprising just a small percent each of the total volume.

With a VUL, the insured needs a significant amount of life coverage to qualify for all the benefits. And with a policy worth several million dollars, the insurance might have to be in the tens of millions—hard to find in any situation. Qualifying also means additional restrictions that could keep the majority of your policy funds out of action for years on end. And the benefit of tax deferral can sometimes be a wash after paying life insurance premiums; however, the distributions from your policy will be income tax free to your beneficiaries upon your death.

The FCV, however, is a niche solution for a very specific type of person. Often uninsurable and given to highly specific needs, the client best suited to this type of policy is a rare one. And few companies across the world even offer it, since it's considered to be a bit aggressive in the way it pursues a tax-advantageous situation. In short, it allows you to enjoy some of the benefits of a conforming VUL (the ability to withdraw tax-free principal before interest, for example) without some of the red tape and hassle that comes with a VUL.

Both the FCV and VUL have a single key advantage over their more flexible, more mainstream cousin, the DVA. Namely, they allow you to pass your wealth on to heirs without being subject to U.S. income tax. Any distributions from a DVA, whether to the insured or the beneficiary, are taxed at ordinary income rates. But for the other two policies, funds are distributed income tax free at the time of death. Depending on the size of the overall estate, these policies may be subject to U.S. estate tax. Always check with a qualified tax professional before making any assumptions.

EXCHANGING YOUR CURRENT U.S. INSURANCE POLICY FOR ONE OFFSHORE

A large majority of Americans who are saving for their retirements may already have a U.S. annuity policy. And often, a large portion of your wealth may already be in such a policy. Well, you should know that is possible for you to move that into a foreign private placement policy.

Under U.S. law (tax code section 1035; Appendix B-14), it's possible to exchange one annuity for another or a life insurance policy for another life insurance or annuity policy. Best of all, you can exchange your U.S. policy for a foreign policy without surrendering the policy or triggering a taxable event.

However, this is a slow process since the U.S. insurers are literally doing everything they can to hold onto your money so they don't lose it. In fact, it is not uncommon for large U.S. insurance carriers to tell you that it is illegal to transfer existing policies abroad or threaten that you may lose your tax benefits by taking this step. Yet if you invest the time and you are insistent, they will eventually transfer the policy.

Here is how the procedure works:

Step 1. You sign an application form with a foreign insurer. At the same time, you assign the current American policy to the foreign insurance company (Appendix B-15).

Step 2. The foreign insurer will surrender your American policy, redeem the funds, and apply them to the underlying account, where they will be invested according to the agreed strategy.

Step 3. Your new private placement policy is then issued.

As always, you should consult a professional before exchanging your existing policy. There will be a few forms involved, but all in all, the process is relatively straightforward, with the possible exception of having to fight with your current insurance company to complete the process.

POLICIES MAY BE COMBINED WITH OTHER TYPES OF STRUCTURES FOR BETTER ESTATE PLANNING AND MORE CUSTOM SOLUTIONS

While a private placement policy is one of the best stand-alone investment solutions available, it doesn't *have* to be on its own. If you already have an existing legal structure in place for your money, the policies covered in this chapter are flexible enough to be included. The structure can serve as either the policy owner or the beneficiary. The possibilities are very interesting. Let's take a look at a few options.

It is possible for a trust, either domestic or foreign, to be made the irrevocable beneficiary of a private placement policy. Many asset protection attorneys believe that the private placement policy is very good for asset protection; however, they may fear that not all of the estate planning goals will be met. So the attorney would prefer to have the trust make the final payouts once the insured person dies. With the trust receiving the payout from the policy, the trust could then distribute the money to the beneficiaries over a few generations rather than just during one lifetime. As you can see, by combining the two structures, you have more flexibility with regard to how your wealth is passed on.

Case Study: A Policy Combined with a Trust— The Stetsons' Wish to Leave a Legacy

Frank and Sally Stetson married in 1959 in a small town in Iowa. Together, they opened a small grocery store in town and their business flourished. Over the course of 30 years, they went on to open 29 grocery stores in the Midwest. They also had four children, and now their family included five grandchildren. In the early 2000s, the Stetsons sold their chain of rural grocery stores to a large European conglomerate that was looking to expand into the U.S. market. The Stetsons, who for years had lived on nice but far-from-extravagant earnings from the profits of their business, now found themselves with a large amount of money. They did not want the money to ruin their children or their grandchildren, but they wanted to make sure their heirs would be able to benefit from their first generation of wealth creation for a long time to come.

The goals of the policy for the Stetsons were:

- They wanted to leave a sustainable nest egg for their children, grandchildren, and future generations, so they wanted a policy with tax-efficient growth for the long-term.
- In the event of their death, they wanted some of the money to be distributed right away and the rest to be held in trust.
- They wanted to make sure the money was protected from any potential lawsuits that may arise in the future.

Here is how a solution was created to meet these goals.

Because the Stetsons had a sizeable amount of liquid savings from the sale of their business, they funded a DVA with one single payment of $20 million.

This particular policy was created using the following parameters (see Figure 6.1):

- Policyholder: The Stetsons
- Person insured: Frank
- Beneficiary: The Stetson Family Trust

The Stetsons' attorney set up the trust so that upon the death of Frank and Sally, each of their four children would receive an annual payment for the remainder of their lifetime. At the age of 25, each grandchild would receive a one-time lump-sum payment. The trust would hold the remainder of the money, and additional payments could be approved by the trustee, in accordance with guidelines specified by the Stetsons. Any future generations would also be able to receive a payout from the trust.

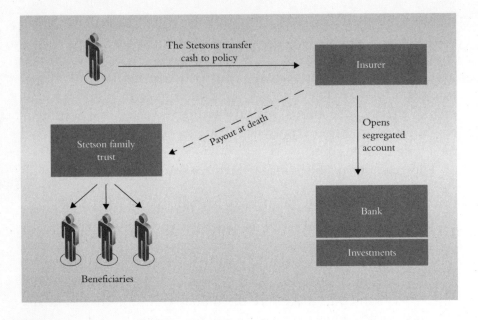

Figure 6.1 Stetson Family Trust with a DVA
Source: NMG International.

Policies can also Be Combined with Life Insurance Trusts

Another example of how the private placement policy can work with another structure can be found with the irrevocable life insurance trust. In this example, a VUL would be owned by the irrevocable life insurance trust, and the same trust would also be the beneficiary of the policy at your death. The advantage to this type of structure is that you would be able to optimize the estate tax situation. Payments from the irrevocable life insurance trust are not subject to estate taxes, but any funds paid into the life insurance trust would trigger a gift tax. However, upon your death, no estate taxes would be due on the trust, but any distribution made from the trust to any of your beneficiaries would be subject to ordinary income tax.

There are many other combinations that are possible with the private placement policies and other structures, such as a private annuity or a charitable remainder unit trust (CRUT). It all depends on the creativity of your professional U.S. tax adviser and his or her ability to look at your overall financial situation and look for ways to find the solutions that will work the best for you.

Should you wish to do this, it's extremely important that in such situations a U.S. tax adviser be involved in order to make sure all the different elements work together as planned.

YOUR ROAD MAP ON WHERE TO GO FROM HERE

In the interest of helping you along in your quest, we've filled the remaining pages of the book with a few appendices that might be of service. These tools, combined with professional assistance and what you've learned so far, should be more than enough to guide you through the process of weighing the options and deciding which type of policy and jurisdiction are right for you.

First, you'll see that we've included a few more case studies of real-life individuals and the policies they created to fit their particular situation. If you haven't found a close approximation of your needs in the case studies so far, you might find one here.

Second, you'll find full, annotated footnotes from this entire volume. If you're interested in picking up where our research left off or finding some useful resources for financial information and economic data, you should take a look.

There's also an extended glossary, which you might notice includes some terms not used in the body of this book. While you may not have seen those terms here, there's a good chance you'll hear them in your first few annuity discussions with attorneys or financial advisers, so we included them to help you prepare.

There's also an extended section on Liechtenstein's law regarding insurers, and some of the different solutions available specifically through that jurisdiction. Since it's a world leader and arguably the best possible jurisdiction for most of our readers, Appendix B-12 will offer a little bit more depth in conceptualizing your policy.

ONE FINAL BIT OF ADVICE . . .

As our final words to you, we offer this: don't discount the unexpected.

Rather than face the threats detailed in this book, it will be easier to just put the book down when you're done and never give it a second thought. Indeed, it can be a bit scary when your mind starts wandering through all the possibilities discussed in these pages. So it's probably tempting to bury your head in the sand like an ostrich and just pray this stuff never happens.

But that's not a viable financial strategy.

It didn't work for people who ignored talk of a bubble in tech stocks or subprime housing, it didn't work for Argentines who never believed the government would confiscate their retirement assets, and it won't work for you.

If the events of the past few years have taught us anything, it's that you *must* be proactive—you must seek the alternatives. The mainstream message will be more wrong than it will be right. And when it's wrong, it isn't the investment banker that suffers. No, he will walk away flush while we're all stuck with worthless stock in our retirement portfolios. Thanks, but no thanks, we say.

Instead, we'd rather do a little bit of homework and go with the best alternative the world has to offer—one that lets us enjoy life knowing our money is well at work, one that meets all of our needs and more, even if no one in our social circle has ever heard of it. When you look outside the box, you'll see there is a world of possibilities.

As Albert Einstein once said, "Chance favors the prepared mind." And as we stare upon our uncertain financial and economic future, at the chances to build wealth and the chances to lose it, we couldn't possibly agree more. So don't discount the unexpected, be prepared, and chances are you'll find that the chips fall in your favor more often than they would have otherwise.

EXAMPLES OF HOW PRIVATE PLACEMENT POLICIES MAY BE USED

Case Studies

Given the multiple ways that private placement policies can be used, we have included a few case studies to show how flexible and varied their uses may be. Some of the stories contained within this book and in this appendix are hypothetical; however, many stories are real examples. We have intentionally used pseudonyms out of respect for personal privacy and confidentiality.

We hope that these examples will assist you in your quest for the right financial solution.

CASE STUDY 1: RUSSELL—YEARS IN THE ICE CREAM BUSINESS PAYS OFF

Russell is a jolly old man much like anyone in his position might be. He began his career driving his ice cream truck around town, selling treats to the local kids. He saved and worked diligently, and eventually opened an ice cream shop in his small town. That was 25 years before he first came to realize he needed to think about growing and protecting his wealth. Now, he had opened two more shops and built a strong brand presence in his small town.

Tourism was on the rise, he explained, and a group had offered to buy him out. Russell wasn't yet ready to retire, but they made a pretty tempting offer, and Russell saw the opportunity to seriously improve his future prospects and elevate his quality of life. A man who never would have believed he would be a millionaire now saw that he had the opportunity.

So, Russell took the offer and made the deal to sell his business.

In the immediate term, Russell was looking for a place to deposit the proceeds of the sale—by far the largest financial transaction of his lifetime. His primary concern was putting the money where it would do the most good for himself and his family and where he could enjoy the full benefit of this newfound wealth. He thought that perhaps he would make some withdrawals 10 or 20 years down the line in order to splurge on some extravagant vacations and perhaps purchase a summer home to enjoy during his golden years. Russell already had separate retirement savings, and he wasn't planning to stop working just yet. He planned on consuming his retirement savings during his lifetime and using the remaining balance from the sale of his business to pass his wealth on to his wife and children once he was gone.

So Russell did not need the income—at least not yet.

Due to the terms of the business deal, Russell would be obligated to stay on for five more years and build a new management team as his ownership shares were gradually bought out. So he wasn't in a hurry to fund everything immediately, and, in fact, he wouldn't have even been able to because he did not have the cash on hand. He would only have the money to fund the policy as his ownership shares were paid out.

Here were the goals that Russell's policy had to meet:

- Make the most out of his newfound wealth so that he could access the money when he wished.

- Fund the balance of the policy over the course of at least five years from the payouts he was receiving from the sale of his business.
- Supplement his existing retirement funds.
- Act as an estate planning vehicle for transferring wealth to his wife and children once he was gone.

The right solution for Russell was a variable universal life (VUL) policy (nonmodified endowment contract [non-MEC]). The policy would allow him to make multiple payments into the policy, and it would allow his family to receive the money income tax free upon his death.

So the VUL non-MEC was created with the following parameters:

- Policyholder: Russell
- Person insured: Russell
- Beneficiary at death of the insured: Russell's wife and children in equal shares

Russell's situation and goals made him a prime candidate for a VUL. The type of policy required him to undergo medical testing, and in order to enjoy the full tax benefits, he had to pay into his policy over the course of seven years. That was just two years beyond the full-term sale of his business, so it wasn't too difficult for him to make the payments over such a period.

Plus, it allowed him to make withdrawals from the principal of his policy when he wanted to without triggering any income taxes. So when he buys a summer home on the lake or takes his family on a cruise in the Mediterranean, he'll be doing so without being taxed for the withdrawal. This would not have been the case if he had selected to use a deferred variable annuity (DVA). Also, unlike the DVA, his heirs will receive their inheritance free of income tax; however, they may still have to pay estate taxes on whatever they receive.

So far, everything has worked out well for Russell. He selected a relatively conservative investment strategy for the money within his policy, and even after the difficult year of 2008 and the market's upswing in 2009, Russell's plan is on track and his policy is growing moderately. The most important thing for him is that he now is able to enjoy peace of mind knowing that his money is protected, invested, and at his disposal should he need it during his lifetime.

CASE STUDY 2: MICHAEL AND SHEILA—THE YOUNG MILLIONAIRES

Michael and Sheila are a high-powered American couple. Each was highly successful in their careers, and yet they were barely in their 30s. They had two young children, and they were settling into their first nice home as a family. They first started to look for a solution to their wealth concerns in 2000.

Michael was a realtor. He had the foresight to realize that his outrageous level of income might not last forever. Together, they could cover all their monthly expenses with a tiny sliver of their income, and—like squirrels saving nuts for the winter—they wanted to divert some of it in case there was a change in their income level in the future.

Even though they were not planning to withdraw funds from the policy, they wanted the flexibility to take money out or to liquidate the plan entirely should the need arise in the future. Their main goal was to build a secure savings over the long term to ensure the care and well-being of their young children.

Due to their combination of high income and careful thriftiness, they already had individual retirement accounts (IRAs) and 401(k)s, savings, and checking, as well as sizable stock accounts. They were both very financially educated and very experienced. Both of them were relatively avid at building and maintaining their wealth. But they expressed the desire for something more, for even more diversification. In addition, Sheila's line of work as a pediatric surgeon made a legal level of asset protection more of a requisite than a bonus. Looking at their entire situation, they needed a policy that would meet their specific goals:

- A great level of international diversification and investment flexibility. These were options they couldn't find in their existing IRAs or traditional stock market accounts.

- Maximum growth for retirement, but also the flexibility to make withdrawals or even liquidate the policy at any point without penalty.
- Long-term fail-safes built into the policy in case they pass on before their children reach adulthood.

The right solution for Michael and Sheila was a DVA. So the DVA was created with the following parameters:

- Policyholders: Michael and Sheila
- Person insured: Joint policy for Michael and Sheila
- Beneficiary at death of the insured: Their children

For their particular situation, the DVA offered the best possible solution. It offers the highest level of flexibility, and it frees them from the hassle of life coverage or long waiting periods. Also, since their main goal was to maximize the investment growth, an additional life insurance rider would have eaten up a large amount of that growth on an annual basis.

But despite the fact that it can be liquidated at a moment's notice (with a tax penalty of 10 percent if they were to surrender the policy prior to age 59½), it's mainly built for the long term, as they desired. Should one of them pass away prematurely, the policy will fall to the spouse. And just in case both pass away before their children reach the age of 18, the policy is designed to pay out a $50,000 annual income to each child. Once they reach the age of 18, the remaining funds would be released to each of the children.

They were also very attracted to the investment flexibility of an offshore variable annuity because it was able to complement their existing portfolios quite nicely. They created a highly customized investment strategy, comprised largely of managed futures, bond funds, and foreign currencies, by using a pool of hand-picked asset managers to handle the actual investment decisions.

Their policy has done extremely well in the time since then, returning over 14 percent each year. Michael and Sheila both admit that their own business hasn't been going quite so well since the crash of the U.S. mortgage market, so they're extremely grateful for the foresight to create this sort of plan while they had the time and the money.

CASE STUDY 3: JOHN AND MARTHA—THE SAILING COUPLE

John and Martha had the grand ambition of sailing around the world.

Thanks to hard work and good fortune, they were both going to be able to retire a few years earlier than they had expected. And since they spent the last two decades chartering sailboats and cruising the Caribbean, the Mediterranean, and even the Indian Ocean, they liked the idea of such a grand adventure.

But—as is the case for so many of us—it wasn't quite so easy.

Together, John and Martha ran a business for most of their professional lives. It was a profitable business, but one where even a minor error could give way to major lawsuits. They trusted the management team they'd hired and trained to carry the business after their retirement, but they simply wanted to be certain that they were protected in case something went wrong. So, regardless of whether they ever set sail, they wanted to be assured that their personal assets were kept clear of any business liabilities.

Additionally, they realized the risk of their endeavor. They were both capable at sea, and they planned on hiring a few deckhands for the voyage; but, again, they wanted to be certain. The youngest two of their five children were still in college, and another was just beginning to get on his feet financially. At the very least, they wanted to offer these three children some income to carry them the rest of the way through adulthood if something on the trip went awry.

Beyond that, John expressed personal concern about the state of the U.S. economy and the dollar's prospects for the future. These concerns were one of the major reasons he began to look for a foreign investment solution. He was quite adamant that the majority of his policy's underlying assets be denominated in a handful of foreign currencies with very little U.S. exposure. The goals for John and Martha were:

- To create a solution that offers the best possible asset protection to guard against any lawsuits involving their business so that personal assets are not placed at risk.

- To aggressively diversify John and Martha's currency base and pare down their U.S. dollar exposure.
- To offer a fail-safe for their trip around the world so that in case something happened to them, their youngest children would be financially secure.

The right solution for John and Martha was a DVA. So the DVA was created with the following parameters:

- Policyholders: John and Martha
- Person insured: Joint policy for John and Martha
- Beneficiary: John and Martha
- Beneficiary at death of the insured: Their children

Diversifying their currency base was no new task. Indeed, it's usually one of the first steps that most American investors pursue.

For John and Martha, this involved an asset manager who specialized in emerging-market bonds, and another who focused on European stocks. As soon as their plan was in place, they began to profit not only from faster-moving emerging markets, but from the rising currencies as well.

Their particular need for asset protection led us to domicile the policy in Liechtenstein, where their savings would be relatively untouchable in most cases. If something happened to them during their trip, the children, as the beneficiaries, would receive immediate access to cash and income. Once their policy was in place, they set off on their sailing adventure and enjoyed the trip without worry.

CASE STUDY 4: AARON AND HIS EX-WIFE

Aaron is an American Israeli in his early 60s living in Miami, Florida. Aaron is an entrepreneur running several businesses and employing approximately 2,000 people mainly in the United States and some in Europe.

When Aaron set out to find a solution to his wealth concerns, he already knew exactly what he wanted. His main concerns were investment diversification, tax deferral, and asset protection. Aaron was divorced and had two children in their early 30s.

On the investment side, Aaron was looking for an international hedge fund portfolio, which he normally could not invest in as an American. Also, the tax consequences would be terrible even if he could due to the passive foreign investment company (PFIC) rules.

Aaron needed a private placement policy to help him reach the following goals:

- Investment flexibility and diversification so that he could invest in a sophisticated hedge fund type portfolio.
- The ability for his investments to grow tax deferred until he needed to take a distribution.
- To ensure that his money was protected in the event of any legal issues with his businesses.

A DVA was the right type of policy for someone like Aaron. So a policy was created with the following parameters:

- Policyholder: Aaron
- Person insured: Aaron
- Beneficiary: Aaron
- Beneficiary at death of the insured: His two children in equal shares

Once the tax-deferred variable annuity was created, Aaron was able to select an asset manager from one of the most sophisticated private banks in Switzerland specializing in hedge fund strategies. Since the insurance company is the owner and investor of the funds, there are no issues due to citizenship and the like, and since the policy was set up to meet the rules for tax deferral under U.S. law, no PFIC rules applied and the funds grew tax deferred.

For asset protection, the policy was established in Liechtenstein, and it was structured in such a way that the assets would be protected, but Aaron would still have a great deal of flexibility. At the time the policy was set up as a standard matter of practice, Aaron was informed about the fraudulent conveyance rules, which require that no bankruptcy or seizure of the policy take place within the first 12 months after the setup of the policy. Aaron confirmed that no creditors were knocking at his door and he could not see where a lawsuit would come from.

About 11 months later, Aaron called the insurance company and he was concerned. It turned out that Aaron's ex-wife was suing him for a substantial amount of money, and she tried to attach the policies that had been set up earlier during the year. Due to the recent creation of the policy, it was unclear if the protection would be solid or if it could be challenged.

It seems that Aaron had shared all the information about his policies with his brother, who, after an argument with Aaron, decided to pass on all the information about the policies and the insurer to Aaron's ex-wife.

There was a substantial amount of money involved, so Aaron's ex-wife hired a law firm in Liechtenstein and took the case to court. Of course, the local court froze the policy in order to first check and clarify the situation. After a short time, however, the policies were released and the ex-wife was sent back home. The court argued that the policy, in the way in which it had been set up, was fully protected and therefore not considered an asset that could be seized. Also, since neither Aaron nor his ex-wife had residency in Liechtenstein and had no assets that could be seized held within the country, the ex-wife had no right to come in front of a court in Liechtenstein.

It goes without saying that Aaron was very happy with the outcome of the policy, especially since the attack happened after only approximately 12 months from the date the policy was created. Of course, this was not the end of Aaron's issues with his ex-wife. She continued to try to freeze other U.S.-based assets that Aaron held. Finally, Aaron and his ex-wife came to a resolution and settled their battle.

Today, Aaron still holds his policies and is living a stress-free life, knowing that he has a great amount of protection should another threat come his way.

APPENDIX B

FURTHER RESOURCES AND READING

The ideas expressed in this book have dramatic implications for those readers who are serious about achieving a secure financial future in the twenty-first century.

We have presented the information about private placement policies and the benefits in a direct and clear way in order make the content useful to nontechnical readers. Within the chapters of the book, we intentionally decided not to delve into how private placement polices are reported or to explain IRS regulations or to focus on the details of asset protection laws in other countries, yet we do feel this information is important.

In this appendix, we have included some of the technical information and website links that provide a variety of the laws, IRS codes, and legal definitions we have mentioned and reference within in the body of the text. These definitions and laws are tedious and dry reading; however, we know that many of you may wish to invest the time to fully understand this information. This is especially true if you are considering a policy in a specific jurisdiction or if you are considering a policy in lieu of another holding structure, such as an offshore corporation and the like.

Most, if not all, of these documents have come from government websites and were the most current documents available when the book went to print. However, government regulations and reporting requirements change regularly and without much warning. Thus, we encourage you not to rely solely on this information and to consult with a legal and/or tax professional about your personal situation before making any financial decisions.

The sections included in this appendix are as follows

B-1: Section 7. Passive Foreign Investment Companies
B-2: IRS Section 957—Controlled Foreign Corporations
B-3: EverBank Contact Information
B-4: Department of the Treasury—Internal Revenue Service Section 8754
B-5: Liechtenstein Supervision Laws
B-6: IRS Form 720
B-7: Foreign Insurance Excise Tax
B-8: TDF 90-22.1 Form
B-9: 26 U.S.C. § 7702—U.S. Code Section 7702: Life Insurance Contract Defined
B-10: Seven-Pay Test VUL—Non-MEC
B-11: Premium Guidelines
B-12: Liechtenstein Insurance Contract Act
B-13: U.S. Liechtenstein TIEA
B-14: IRS Section 1035
B-15: 1035 Assignment Letter

B-1: SECTION 7. PASSIVE FOREIGN INVESTMENT COMPANIES

.01 In General

Section 1(h)(11)(C)(iii) of the Code excludes PFICs from the definition of qualified foreign corporation. As a result, a dividend (including an excess distribution) from a foreign corporation that is a PFIC or that is not a PFIC in the current taxable year but was a PFIC in the preceding taxable year is not qualified dividend income.

Similarly, amounts included in a shareholder's gross income under sections 1293(a) (in the case of a shareholder that has made a QEF election) or 1296 (in the case of a shareholder that has made a mark to market election) are not qualified dividend income.

.02 Determination of PFIC Status

As noted above in section 3.02(4), some of the rules for determining whether a foreign corporation is a PFIC operate on a shareholder-by-shareholder basis. Therefore, a foreign corporation may be treated as a PFIC with respect to some shareholders but not others. Thus, for purposes of section 1(h)(11), the result of an analysis of whether a foreign corporation is a PFIC, and therefore whether dividends from that corporation are for that reason excluded from qualified dividend income, may be different for shareholders of the same foreign corporation.

A determination of whether a foreign corporation was a PFIC in the previous taxable year also should be made on a shareholder-by-shareholder basis if the shareholder of the foreign corporation was a shareholder in the previous taxable year. For example, a foreign corporation that was a PFIC under the income test or the asset test of section 1297(a) of the Code for one year of a shareholder's holding period under certain circumstances may be a PFIC with respect to that shareholder even though it may not meet the income or asset tests in subsequent years and notwithstanding that the foreign corporation may not be a PFIC with respect to other shareholders.

Section 1298(b)(1). To the extent a foreign corporation is a PFIC with respect to a shareholder, dividends received by that shareholder are not qualified dividend income.

Source: Internal Revenue Bulletin: 2004-44, www.irs.gov/irb/2004-44_IRB/ar09.html#d0e3449.

B-2: IRS SECTION 957—CONTROLLED FOREIGN CORPORATIONS

Controlled Foreign Corporation. Section 957 of the Internal Revenue Code defines a foreign corporation as being "controlled" if more than 50 percent of the total combined voting power of all classes of stock of such corporation entitled to vote, or more than 50 percent of the value of all its outstanding stock, is owned (directly, indirectly, or constructively) by U.S. shareholders on any day during the foreign corporation's tax year. A U.S. shareholder for purposes of determining control is defined as a "U.S. person" (see definition below) owning 10 percent or more of the foreign corporation's voting stock. For purposes of these statistics, a foreign corporation was "controlled" only if a single U.S. corporation satisfied the ownership requirements for an uninterrupted period of at least 30 days. These are the only foreign corporations for which complete Form 5471 filings are required. U.S corporations may also control a CFC through a partnership where the U.S. corporation is the controlling partner. To the extent possible, these CFCs have also been included in these statistics.

Country of incorporation. The country of incorporation is the country under whose laws the CFC is legally created. The CFC's country of incorporation is not necessarily the principal place of business. For Tax Year 2004, 1,728 CFCs (2.3 percent) reported a principal place of business that differed from the reported country of incorporation.

Current earnings and profits. "Current earnings and profits" represent the difference between total earnings and profits of the foreign corporation at the end of the current year (before reduction by dividends paid during the year) and the accumulated earnings and profits of the corporation at the beginning of the year. Although current earnings and profits typically are an after-tax measure of profits, they are shown in these statistics both before and after taxes. "Earnings and profits" is a tax concept referring to the economic capacity of a corporation to make a distribution to shareholders that is not a return on capital. The term "earnings and profits" is not specifically defined in the Internal Revenue Code. In those instances where current earnings and profits were not reported for the foreign corporation, net income per books was used in place of missing earnings and profits.

Distributions out of earnings and profits. Distributions out of earnings and profits represent payments to shareholders from the foreign corporation's pool of earnings and profits. A distribution comes first from current earnings and profits and then from accumulated earnings and profits. Distributions may be from previously taxed earnings and profits or non–previously taxed earnings and profits.

Income taxes. CFCs reported income, war profits, and excess profits taxes paid or accrued to any foreign country or U.S. Possession as income tax for their annual accounting period.

SOURCE: www.irs.gov/taxstats/bustaxstats/article/0,,id=212772,00 .html.

B-3: EVERBANK CONTACT INFORMATION

About EverBank: EverBank Direct is the online banking channel of Florida-based EverBank. Operating nationally by telephone, mail, and Internet, EverBank has become a recognized leader in consumer direct banking and lending across America. EverBank also provides access to global markets through its World Markets department.

About EverBank Financial Corporation: EverBank Financial Corporation, and its EverBank subsidiaries, is a privately held thrift holding company headquartered in Jacksonville, Florida, offering innovative banking, lending, and investment products and services of exceptional value. In 2009, EverBank assets and deposits grew to nearly $8.0 billion and $6.4 billion, respectively.

B-4: DEPARTMENT OF THE TREASURY—INTERNAL REVENUE SERVICE SECTION 8754

Internal Revenue Code section 8754 contains final regulations relating to the federal income tax treatment of certain annuity contracts. The regulations determine which of these contracts are taxed as debt instruments for purposes of the original issue discount provisions of the Internal Revenue Code. The regulations provide needed guidance to owners and issuers of these contracts.

To review the full document, please visit www.irs.ustreas.gov/pub/irs-regs/td8754.pdf.

B-5: LIECHTENSTEIN SUPERVISION LAWS

This law describes the organization and content of the supervision of insurance undertakings and, in particular, has the object of protecting policyholders and maintaining confidence in the Liechtenstein insurance and financial sector.

To review the full document, please visit www.pgr.li/cd/en/Teil_3/law_on_supervision_01.html.

B-6: IRS FORM 720

This IRS form must be completed and filed when you purchase the annuity in order to pay the U.S. government excise tax on the foreign policy.

To review the full document, please visit www.irs.gov/pub/irs-pdf/f720.pdf.

B-7: FOREIGN INSURANCE EXCISE TAX

Introduction

Internal Revenue Code § 4371 requires all of the following three elements for the foreign insurance excise tax to apply. They are:

1. A policy of insurance,
2. Insurance of a United States risk, and
3. Policy issued by a foreign insurer or reinsurer.

Policy of Insurance

A policy of insurance may include a policy of reinsurance, an indemnity bond, or an annuity contract. Generally, a policy is the printed document issued by the insurer presented to the insured, which contains the terms of the insurance contract. This document is sometimes referred to as a **treaty**. When the insurer transfers the same risks to another insurer, reinsurance has occurred and the second insurer is termed the **reinsurer**.

Indemnity Bond

An indemnity bond is a contract under which the surety party promises to reimburse a third party, called the obligee, for losses it sustained as a result of the failure of the principal party, called the obligor, to perform under its contract with the obligee.

Annuity Contract

An annuity contract is a contract that provides for periodic payments starting from a certain date and continuing for a fixed period or for the life of the annuitant.

Insurance of a United States Risk

United States risk is defined follows:

1. For life insurance, sickness and accident insurance, and annuity contracts, the policy or contract must be with respect to the

life or hazards to the person of a **citizen or resident of the United States**.

2. For casualty insurance or indemnity bonds, the definition depends upon the residency of the insured (in the case of a corporation or partnership, the country in which it is created or organized).

   - For a United States insured, the policy must cover risks wholly or partly within the United States.
   - For a foreign insured, the insured must be engaged in a trade or business within the United States and the covered risks must be **wholly** within the United States. See IRC § 4372.

Policy Issued by a Foreign Insurer or Reinsurer

The policy of insurance must be issued by a foreign insurer or reinsurer. A foreign insurer or reinsurer is defined under I.R.C. § 4372(a) as a nonresident alien individual, a foreign partnership, or a foreign corporation.

Liability for Tax

While the Service generally holds the person making the premium payments liable for the tax, the liability is joint and several. Under I.R.C. § 4374 the tax may be imposed tax on any of the following persons:

- The insured, sometimes referred to as the beneficiary,
- The policyholder, if that person is someone other than the insured,
- The insurance company, or
- The broker obtaining the insurance.

Internal Revenue Code § 4372(d) further defines insured to include any of the following:

- A domestic corporation or partnership, or an individual resident of the United States, or
- A foreign corporation, foreign partnership, or nonresident individual engaged in a trade or business within the United States.

Computation of the Tax Due

The applicable tax rate depends directly on the type of insurance coverage provided in the contract. The table below reflects the rate to be imposed based on the type of coverage in the insurance contract.

Type of Coverage	Rate
Casualty insurance or indemnity bonds	4%
Life insurance, sickness and accident policies or annuity contracts	1%
Reinsurance	1%

Once the tax rate is determined, it is to be applied to the amount of the premiums paid. The amount of premiums paid is defined in Treas. Reg. § 46.4371-3(b) as "the consideration paid for assuming and carrying the risk or obligation [of the insured]." This is the gross amount, not the net amount.

SOURCE: www.irs.gov/businesses/small/article/0,,id=186963,00 .html#chp01.

B-8: TDF 90-22.1 FORM

Each United States person who has a financial interest in or signature or other authority over any foreign financial accounts, including bank, securities, or other types of financial accounts, in a foreign country, if the aggregate value of these financial accounts exceeds $10,000 at any time during the calendar year, must report that relationship each calendar year by filing this report with the Department of the Treasury on or before June 30 of the succeeding year.

There are differing legal opinions as to whether an offshore private placement policy would be considered a foreign financial account. However, it is best to be safe and, thus, it is recommended that you file this form if you establish an offshore policy.

To review the full document, please visit www.irs.gov/pub/ irs-pdf/f90221.pdf.

B-9: 26 U.S.C. § 7702—US CODE SECTION 7702: LIFE INSURANCE CONTRACT DEFINED

(a) General rule—For purposes of this title, the term "life insurance contract" means any contract which is a life insurance contract under the applicable law, but only if such contract
(1) meets the cash value accumulation test of subsection (b), or
(2) (A) meets the guideline premium requirements of subsection (c), and
(B) falls within the cash value corridor of subsection (d).
(b) Cash value accumulation test for subsection (a)(1)
(1) In general
A contract meets the cash value accumulation test of this subsection if, by the terms of the contract, the cash surrender value of such contract may not at any time exceed the net single premium which would have to be paid at such time to fund future benefits under the contract.
(2) Rules for applying paragraph (1)
Determinations under paragraph (1) shall be made
(A) on the basis of interest at the greater of an annual effective rate of 4 percent or the rate or rates guaranteed on issuance of the contract,
(B) on the basis of the rules of subparagraph (B)(i) (and, in the case of qualified additional benefits, subparagraph (B)(ii)) of subsection (c)(3), and
(C) by taking into account under subparagraphs (A) and (D) of subsection (e)(1) only current and future death benefits and qualified additional benefits.
(c) Guideline premium requirements
For purposes of this section
(1) In general
A contract meets the guideline premium requirements of this subsection if the sum of the premiums paid under such contract does not at any time exceed the guideline premium limitation as of such time.
(2) Guideline premium limitation

The term "guideline premium limitation" means, as of any date, the greater of

(A) the guideline single premium, or

(B) the sum of the guideline level premiums to such date.

(3) Guideline single premium

(A) In general

The term "guideline single premium" means the premium at issue with respect to future benefits under the contract.

(B) Basis on which determination is made

The determination under subparagraph (A) shall be based on

(i) reasonable mortality charges which meet the requirements (if any) prescribed in regulations and which (except as provided in regulations) do not exceed the mortality charges specified in the prevailing commissioners' standard tables (as defined in section 807(d)(5)) as of the time the contract is issued,

(ii) any reasonable charges (other than mortality charges) which (on the basis of the company's experience, if any, with respect to similar contracts) are reasonably expected to be actually paid, and

(iii) interest at the greater of an annual effective rate of 6 percent or the rate or rates guaranteed on issuance of the contract.

(C) When determination made

Except as provided in subsection (f)(7), the determination under subparagraph (A) shall be made as of the time the contract is issued.

(D) Special rules for subparagraph (B)(ii)

(i) Charges not specified in the contract

If any charge is not specified in the contract, the amount taken into account under subparagraph (B)(ii) for such charge shall be zero.

(ii) New companies, etc.

If any company does not have adequate experience for purposes of the determination under subparagraph (B)(ii), to the extent provided in regulations, such determination shall be made on the basis of the industry-wide experience.

(4) Guideline level premium

The term "guideline level premium" means the level annual amount, payable over a period not ending before the insured attains age 95, computed on the same basis as the guideline single premium, except that paragraph (3)(B)(iii) shall be applied by substituting "4 percent" for "6 percent."

(d) Cash value corridor for purposes of subsection (a)(2)(B)

For purposes of this section

(1) In general

A contract falls within the cash value corridor of this subsection if the death benefit under the contract at any time is not less than the applicable percentage of the cash surrender value.

(2) Applicable percentage

In the case of an insured with an attained age at the beginning of the contract year of:		The Applicable percentage shall decrease by a ratable portion for each full year:	
More than:	But not:	From:	To:
age 0	age 40	250	250
age 40	age 45	250	215
age 45	age 50	215	185
age 50	age 55	185	150
age 55	age 60	150	130
age 60	age 65	130	120
age 65	age 70	120	115
age 70	age 75	115	105
age 75	age 90	105	105
age 90	age 95	105	100.

(e) Computational rules

(1) In general

For purposes of this section (other than subsection (d))

(A) the death benefit (and any qualified additional benefit) shall be deemed not to increase,

(B) the maturity date, including the date on which any benefit described in subparagraph (C) is payable, shall be deemed to be no earlier than the day on which the insured attains age 95, and no later than the day on which the insured attains age 100,

(C) the death benefits shall be deemed to be provided until the maturity date determined by taking into account subparagraph (B), and

(D) the amount of any endowment benefit (or sum of endowment benefits, including any cash surrender value on the maturity date determined by taking into account subparagraph (B)) shall be deemed not to exceed the least amount payable as a death benefit at any time under the contract.

(2) Limited increases in death benefit permitted

Notwithstanding paragraph (1)(A)

(A) for purposes of computing the guideline level premium, an increase in the death benefit which is provided in the contract may be taken into account but only to the extent necessary to prevent a decrease in the excess of the death benefit over the cash surrender value of the contract,

(B) for purposes of the cash value accumulation test, the increase described in subparagraph (A) may be taken into account if the contract will meet such test at all times assuming that the net level reserve (determined as if level annual premiums were paid for the contract over a period not ending before the insured attains age 95) is substituted for the net single premium, and

(C) for purposes of the cash value accumulation test, the death benefit increases may be taken into account if the contract

   (i) has an initial death benefit of $5,000 or less and a maximum death benefit of $25,000 or less,

   (ii) provides for a fixed predetermined annual increase not to exceed 10 percent of the initial death benefit or 8 percent of the death benefit at the end of the preceding year, and

    (iii) was purchased to cover payment of burial expenses or in connection with prearranged funeral expenses.

For purposes of subparagraph (C), the initial death benefit of a contract shall be determined by treating all contracts issued to the same contract owner as 1 contract.

(f) Other definitions and special rules

  For purposes of this section

  (1) Premiums paid

    (A) In general

      The term "premiums paid" means the premiums paid under the contract less amounts (other than amounts includible in gross income) to which section 72(e) applies and less any excess premiums with respect to which there is a distribution described in subparagraph (B) or (E) of paragraph (7) and any other amounts received with respect to the contract which are specified in regulations.

    (B) Treatment of certain premiums returned to policyholder

      If, in order to comply with the requirements of subsection (a)(2)(A), any portion of any premium paid during any contract year is returned by the insurance company (with interest) within 60 days after the end of a contract year, the amount so returned (excluding interest) shall be deemed to reduce the sum of the premiums paid under the contract during such year.

    (C) Interest returned includible in gross income

      Notwithstanding the provisions of section 72(e), the amount of any interest returned as provided in subparagraph (B) shall be includible in the gross income of the recipient.

  (2) Cash values

    (A) Cash surrender value

      The cash surrender value of any contract shall be its cash value determined without regard to any surrender charge, policy loan, or reasonable termination dividends.

(B) Net surrender value

The net surrender value of any contract shall be determined with regard to surrender charges but without regard to any policy loan.

(3) Death benefit

The term "death benefit" means the amount payable by reason of the death of the insured (determined without regard to any qualified additional benefits).

(4) Future benefits

The term "future benefits" means death benefits and endowment benefits.

(5) Qualified additional benefits

(A) In general

The term "qualified additional benefits" means any –

(i) guaranteed insurability,

(ii) accidental death or disability benefit,

(iii) family term coverage,

(iv) disability waiver benefit, or

(v) other benefit prescribed under regulations.

(B) Treatment of qualified additional benefits

For purposes of this section, qualified additional benefits shall not be treated as future benefits under the contract, but the charges for such benefits shall be treated as future benefits.

(C) Treatment of other additional benefits

In the case of any additional benefit which is not a qualified additional benefit

(i) such benefit shall not be treated as a future benefit, and

(ii) any charge for such benefit which is not prefunded shall not be treated as a premium.

(6) Premium payments not disqualifying contract

The payment of a premium which would result in the sum of the premiums paid exceeding the guideline premium limitation shall be disregarded for purposes of subsection (a)(2) if the amount of such premium does not exceed the amount necessary to prevent the termination of the contract on or before the end of the contract year (but only if the contract will have no cash surrender value at the end of such extension period).

(7) Adjustments

  (A) In general

    If there is a change in the benefits under (or in other terms of) the contract which was not reflected in any previous determination or adjustment made under this section, there shall be proper adjustments in future determinations made under this section.

  (B) Rule for certain changes during first 15 years. If

    (i) a change described in subparagraph (A) reduces benefits under the contract,

    (ii) the change occurs during the 15-year period beginning on the issue date of the contract, and

    (iii) a cash distribution is made to the policyholder as a result of such change, section 72 (other than subsection (e)(5) thereof) shall apply to such cash distribution to the extent it does not exceed the recapture ceiling determined under subparagraph (C) or (D) (whichever applies).

  (C) Recapture ceiling where change occurs during first 5 years

    If the change referred to in subparagraph (B)(ii) occurs during the 5-year period beginning on the issue date of the contract, the recapture ceiling is

    (i) in the case of a contract to which subsection (a)(1) applies, the excess of

      (I) the cash surrender value of the contract, immediately before the reduction, over

      (II) the net single premium (determined under subsection (b)), immediately after the reduction, or

    (ii) in the case of a contract to which subsection (a)(2) applies, the greater of

      (I) the excess of the aggregate premiums paid under the contract, immediately before the reduction, over the guideline premium limitation for the contract (determined under subsection (c)(2), taking into account the adjustment described in subparagraph (A)), or

      (II) the excess of the cash surrender value of the contract, immediately before the reduction,

over the cash value corridor of subsection (d)
(determined immediately after the reduction).

(D)   Recapture ceiling where change occurs after 5th year
and before 16th year
If the change referred to in subparagraph (B) occurs
after the 5-year period referred to under subparagraph
(C), the recapture ceiling is the excess of the cash surrender value of the contract, immediately before the
reduction, over the cash value corridor of subsection
(d) (determined immediately after the reduction and
whether or not subsection (d) applies to the contract).

(E)   Treatment of certain distributions made in anticipation of benefit reductions
Under regulations prescribed by the Secretary, subparagraph (B) shall apply also to any distribution made
in anticipation of a reduction in benefits under the
contract. For purposes of the preceding sentence,
appropriate adjustments shall be made in the provisions
of subparagraphs (C) and (D); and any distribution
which reduces the cash surrender value of a contract
and which is made within 2 years before a reduction
in benefits under the contract shall be treated as made
in anticipation of such reduction.

(8) Correction of errors
If the taxpayer establishes to the satisfaction of the Secretary
that:

(A)   the requirements described in subsection (a) for any contract year were not satisfied due to reasonable error, and

(B)   reasonable steps are being taken to remedy the error,
the Secretary may waive the failure to satisfy such
requirements.

(9) Special rule for variable life insurance contracts
In the case of any contract which is a variable contract (as
defined in section 817), the determination of whether such
contract meets the requirements of subsection (a) shall be made
whenever the death benefits under such contract change but
not less frequently than once during each 12-month period.

(g)   Treatment of contracts which do not meet subsection
(a) test

(1) Income inclusion

    (A) In general

        If at any time any contract which is a life insurance contract under the applicable law does not meet the definition of life insurance contract under subsection (a), the income on the contract for any taxable year of the policyholder shall be treated as ordinary income received or accrued by the policyholder during such year.

    (B) Income on the contract

        For purposes of this paragraph, the term "income on the contract" means, with respect to any taxable year of the policyholder, the excess of

        (i) the sum of

            (I) the increase in the net surrender value of the contract during the taxable year, and

            (II) the cost of life insurance protection provided under the contract during the taxable year, over

        (ii) the premiums paid (as defined in subsection (f)(1)) under the contract during the taxable year.

    (C) Contracts which cease to meet definition

        If, during any taxable year of the policyholder, a contract which is a life insurance contract under the applicable law ceases to meet the definition of life insurance contract under subsection (a), the income on the contract for all prior taxable years shall be treated as received or accrued during the taxable year in which such cessation occurs.

    (D) Cost of life insurance protection

        For purposes of this paragraph, the cost of life insurance protection provided under the contract shall be the lesser of

        (i) the cost of individual insurance on the life of the insured as determined on the basis of uniform premiums (computed on the basis of 5–year age brackets) prescribed by the Secretary by regulations, or

        (ii) the mortality charge (if any) stated in the contract.

(2) Treatment of amount paid on death of insured

    If any contract which is a life insurance contract under the applicable law does not meet the definition of life insurance contract under subsection (a), the excess of the amount paid by the reason of the death of the insured over the net surrender value of the contract shall be deemed to be paid under a life insurance contract for purposes of section 101 and subtitle B.

(3) Contract continues to be treated as insurance contract

If any contract which is a life insurance contract under the applicable law does not meet the definition of life insurance contract under subsection (a), such contract shall, notwithstanding such failure, be treated as an insurance contract for purposes of this title.

(h) Endowment contracts receive same treatment

(1) In general

References in subsections (a) and (g) to a life insurance contract shall be treated as including references to a contract which is an endowment contract under the applicable law.

(2) Definition of endowment contract

For purposes of this title (other than paragraph (1)), the term "endowment contract" means a contract which is an endowment contract under the applicable law and which meets the requirements of subsection (a).

(i) Transitional rule for certain 20-pay contracts

(1) In general

In the case of a qualified 20-pay contract, this section shall be applied by substituting "3 percent" for "4 percent" in subsection (b)(2).

(2) Qualified 20-pay contract

For purposes of paragraph (1), the term "qualified 20-pay contract" means any contract which

(A) requires at least 20 nondecreasing annual premium payments, and

(B) is issued pursuant to an existing plan of insurance.

(3) Existing plan of insurance

For purposes of this subsection, the term "existing plan of insurance" means, with respect to any contract, any plan of insurance which was filed by the company issuing such contract in 1 or more States before September 28, 1983, and is on file in the appropriate State for such contract.

(j) Certain church self-funded death benefit plans treated as life insurance

    (1) In general

        In determining whether any plan or arrangement described in paragraph (2) is a life insurance contract, the requirement of subsection (a) that the contract be a life insurance contract under applicable law shall not apply.

    (2) Description

        For purposes of this subsection, a plan or arrangement is described in this paragraph if

        (A) such plan or arrangement provides for the payment of benefits by reason of the death of the individuals covered under such plan or arrangement, and

        (B) such plan or arrangement is provided by a church for the benefit of its employees and their beneficiaries, directly or through an organization described in section 414(e)(3)(A) or an organization described in section 414(e)(3)(B)(ii).

    (3) Definitions

        For purposes of this subsection

        (A) Church—The term "church" means a church or a convention or association of churches.

        (B) Employee—The term "employee" includes an employee described in section 414(e)(3)(B).

(k) Regulations

    The Secretary shall prescribe such regulations as may be necessary or appropriate to carry out the purposes of this section.

SOURCE: http://codes.lp.findlaw.com/uscode/26/F/79/7702.

B-10: SEVEN-PAY TEST VUL—NON-MEC

The seven-pay test determines whether a life insurance policy qualifies as a nonmodified endowment contract (Non-MEC) or as a modified endowment contract (MEC). The seven-pay test is set forth in section 7702A(b).

To review the full document, please visit www.usaa.com/inet/ent_utils/McStaticPages?key=advice_what_is_modified_endowment_contract.

B-11: PREMIUM GUIDELINES

Page 7
December 15, 2009

Attachment B
Guideline Premium Test illustration

Limit on Mortality (1 = Current / 2 = 2001CSO)	1
Initial "Set-up Fee"	1.50%
Annual Management Fee	0.35%
Assumed Asset Earned Rate	6.00%
7702 Test (1= CVAT/2 = GP/CVC)	2
Iinitial Premium	15,000,000
Initial Death Benefit	41,534,694

Duration	Beginning-of-Year AV	Cost of Insurance	Earnings	End-of-Year AV	Death Benefit
	14,775,000				
1	14,775,000	287,736	818,530	15,305,795	41,534,694
2	15,305,795	310,990	847,206	15,842,011	41,534,694
3	15,842,011	331,055	876,369	16,387,325	41,534,694
4	16,387,325	350,594	906,075	16,942,806	41,534,694
5	16,942,806	370,016	936,363	17,509,153	41,534,694
6	17,509,153	389,531	967,259	18,086,880	41,534,694
7	18,086,880	409,010	998,800	18,676,670	41,534,694
8	18,676,670	428,313	1,031,032	19,279,389	41,534,694
9	19,279,389	447,280	1,064,014	19,896,122	41,534,694
10	19,896,122	465,728	1,097,817	20,528,212	41,534,694
11	20,528,212	483,768	1,132,511	21,176,955	41,534,694
12	21,176,955	502,700	1,168,095	21,842,350	41,534,694
13	21,842,350	523,921	1,204,491	22,522,921	41,534,694
14	22,522,921	548,595	1,241,549	23,215,875	41,534,694
15	23,215,875	577,656	1,279,059	23,917,278	41,534,694
16	23,917,278	611,820	1,316,758	24,622,216	41,534,694
17	24,622,216	651,626	1,354,338	25,324,928	41,534,694
18	25,324,928	697,472	1,391,451	26,018,908	41,534,694
19	26,018,908	749,681	1,427,711	26,696,938	41,534,694
20	26,696,938	808,599	1,462,691	27,351,030	41,534,694
21	27,351,030	869,790	1,496,190	27,977,430	41,534,694
22	27,977,430	928,024	1,528,291	28,577,698	41,534,694
23	28,577,698	983,335	1,559,082	29,153,445	41,534,694
24	29,153,445	1,035,562	1,588,660	29,706,543	41,534,694
25	29,706,543	1,084,498	1,617,146	30,239,191	41,534,694
26	30,239,191	1,129,857	1,644,677	30,754,011	41,534,694
27	30,754,011	1,171,235	1,671,427	31,254,203	41,534,694
28	31,254,203	1,208,040	1,697,608	31,743,771	41,534,694
29	31,743,771	1,239,400	1,723,497	32,227,869	41,534,694
30	32,227,869	1,264,015	1,749,458	32,713,312	41,534,694
31	32,713,312	1,279,941	1,775,985	33,209,356	41,534,694
32	33,209,356	1,284,228	1,803,770	33,728,897	41,534,694
33	33,728,897	1,272,372	1,833,794	34,290,318	41,534,694
34	34,290,318	1,237,407	1,867,490	34,920,401	41,534,694
35	34,920,401	1,168,431	1,906,986	35,658,956	41,534,694
36	35,658,956	1,048,149	1,955,511	36,566,318	41,534,694
37	36,566,318	848,717	2,018,044	37,735,645	41,534,694
38	37,735,645	524,588	2,102,425	39,313,482	41,534,694
39	39,313,482	0	2,221,212	41,534,694	41,534,694

B-12: LIECHTENSTEIN INSURANCE CONTRACT ACT

The Liechtenstein Insurance Contract Act regulates the relationship between the insurer and the policy holder. It applies to all insurance and annuity policies under Liechtenstein law. Specifically, Articles 77 to 81 determine under what circumstances the policy is protected from seizure and bankruptcy and this defines the asset protection.

To review the full document, please visit www.finanzmarktaufsicht .li/?node=234&page_id=295#insurance.

Note: Once on this page, reference the PDF titled Law 16 May 2001 on Insurance Contracts (Insurance Contract Act, ICA).

B-13: US LIECHTENSTEIN TIEA

This document outlines the agreement between the government of the United States of America and the government of the Principality of Liechtenstein on tax cooperation and the exchange of information relating to taxes.

To review the full document, please visit www.oecd.org/dataoecd/ 8/1/41818936.pdf.

B-14: IRS SECTION 1035

Part I

Section 1035.--Certain Exchanges of Insurance Policies

26 CFR 1.1035-1: Certain exchanges of insurance policies.
(Also Part I, §§ 72, 1031)

NOTICE 2003-51

SECTION 1—PURPOSE

    This Notice addresses the taxation of certain tax-free exchanges of annuity contracts under § 72(e) and § 1035 of the Internal Revenue Code. This Notice announces that Treasury and the Service are considering whether to exercise the authority granted under § 72(e)(11) to promulgate regulations that would prescribe the tax treatment of these transactions. This Notice provides interim guidance regarding the tax treatment of these transactions. Finally, this Notice requests comments regarding the appropriate application of § 72(e)(11) to these transactions.

SECTION 2 — BACKGROUND

    Section 1035(a)(3) provides that no gain or loss shall be recognized on the exchange of an annuity contract for another annuity contract. Section 1.1035-1 of the Income Tax Regulations provides that "the exchange, without recognition of gain or loss, of an annuity contract for another annuity contract under § 1035(a)(3) is limited to cases where the same person or persons are the obligee or obligees under the contract received in the exchange as under the original contract."

    The legislative history of § 1035 states that exchange treatment is appropriate for "individuals who have merely exchanged one insurance policy for another better suited to their needs and who have not actually realized gain." H.R. Rep. No. 1337, 83d Cong., 2d Sess. 81 (1954). In *Conway v. Commissioner*, 111 T.C. 350 (1998), *acq.*, 1999-2 C.B. xvi, the Tax Court held that the direct exchange by an insurance company of a portion of an existing annuity contract to an unrelated insurance company for a new annuity contract was a tax-free exchange under § 1035. In that case, the transfer was made directly from the first insurance company to the unrelated insurance company, and none of the assets transferred in the transaction were received by the taxpayer.

    Section 1035(d)(2) cross-references § 1031 for the rules to determine the basis of property acquired in a § 1035 exchange. Section 1031(d) provides that property acquired in a § 1035 exchange has the same basis as that of the property exchanged, decreased by the amount of any money received by the taxpayer and increased by any gain (or decreased by any loss) recognized by the taxpayer on the exchange. Revenue Ruling 2003-76, 2003-33 I.R.B. __, addresses a transaction in which a taxpayer transfers a portion of the cash value of an existing contract to a new insurance company in exchange for a new annuity contract (commonly referred to as "partial exchanges"). Rev. Rul. 2003-76 holds that the basis under § 1031 and investment in the contract under § 72 of the surviving contract immediately before the exchange is allocated ratably between the surviving contract and the newly issued contract.

Section 72(e) governs the federal tax treatment of distributions from an annuity contract. Section 72(e)(11) provides anti-abuse rules applicable to transactions governed by § 72(e). Section 72(e)(11)(B) grants the Secretary broad authority to publish regulations as necessary "to prevent avoidance of the purposes of [§ 72(e)]."

Section 72(q)(1) imposes a 10 percent penalty on withdrawals from, or surrenders of, annuity contracts. Section 72(q)(2) provides that distributions from an annuity contract will not be subject to the 10 percent penalty if the distribution is made after the taxpayer attains age 59-1/2, if the distribution is made on or after the death of the annuity holder, if the distribution is attributable to the taxpayer's becoming disabled, or if other conditions not relevant here are satisfied.

SECTION 3 — TREATMENT OF CERTAIN PARTIAL EXCHANGES

Treasury and the IRS are concerned that some taxpayers may enter into a transaction similar to the transaction at issue in *Conway* (commonly referred to as a "partial exchange") to reduce or avoid the tax that would otherwise be imposed by § 72(e)(2). For example, if a taxpayer withdraws $100 from an annuity contract with a cash surrender value of $200 and investment in the contract of $80, the entire $100 of the withdrawal would be included in income pursuant to § 72(e)(2). However, if that same taxpayer assigned 50 percent of the cash surrender value of the annuity contract in a partial exchange, such that the cash surrender value of each contract after the exchange was $100 and the investment in each contract after the exchange was $40, and then surrendered either the existing annuity contract or the new annuity contract, under § 72(e)(2) only $60 would be included in income and $40 would be excluded as a return of investment in the contract.

Treasury and the Service are considering whether to exercise the regulatory authority of § 72(e)(11) to address the transaction described above to assure that such transactions do not become a vehicle for avoiding the rules of § 72(e). In particular, Treasury and the Service are considering whether such regulations should provide rules for determining when a partial exchange of an annuity contract followed by the surrender of, or distributions from, either the surviving annuity contract or the new annuity contract should be presumed to have been entered into for tax avoidance purposes. Specifically, Treasury and the Service are considering whether to treat surrenders or distributions that occur within 24 months of the date on which the partial exchange was completed as presumptively entered into for tax avoidance purposes. However, Treasury and the Service believe that taxpayers should be provided the opportunity to rebut any presumption by demonstrating that the surrender or withdrawal was not contemplated at the time the partial exchange was completed. Treasury and the Service are considering whether to treat any surrender or distribution that is not subject to the 10 percent penalty tax imposed by § 72(q)(1) because it is described in § 72(q)(2) as successfully rebutting any presumption. In addition, Treasury and the Service are considering whether other events, such as the safe harbors set forth in § 1.121-3T(e), for divorce, loss of employment and other similar events, should be treated as successfully rebutting any presumption.

SECTION 4 — INTERIM GUIDANCE

Pending the publication of final regulations, the Service, using general principles of tax law, will consider all the facts and circumstances to determine whether a partial exchange and a subsequent withdrawal from, or surrender of, either the surviving annuity contract or the new annuity contract within 24 months of the date on which the partial exchange was completed should be treated as an integrated transaction, and thus whether the two contracts should be viewed as a single contract to determine the tax treatment of a surrender or withdrawal under § 72(e). *See Helvering v. LeGeirse*, 312 U.S. 531 (1941) (concluding that, in substance, annuity contracts and the life insurance contracts purchased by the taxpayer were integrated contracts). However, if a taxpayer demonstrates that one of the conditions of § 72(q)(2), or any other similar life event, such as a divorce or the loss of employment, occurred between the partial exchange and the surrender or distribution, and that the surrender or distribution was not contemplated at the time of the partial exchange, the taxpayer will not be treated as having entered into the partial exchange and the surrender or distribution for tax avoidance purposes.

SECTION 5 — REQUEST FOR COMMENTS

Treasury and the Service request comments regarding the need for regulations under § 72(e)(11) to prevent the use of partial exchange transactions as a means of avoiding the tax imposed by § 72(e). In addition, Treasury and the Service request comments regarding whether the principles outlined in Section 3 appropriately address Treasury's and the Service's concern without significantly limiting the ability of taxpayers to use partial exchanges to acquire annuity contracts that "are better suited to their needs" as contemplated by Congress. Treasury and the Service also request comments regarding any other similar transactions that any regulations under § 72(e)(11) should address.

DRAFTING INFORMATION

The principal author of this notice is Ann H. Logan of the Office of Associate Chief Counsel (Financial Institutions and Products). For further information regarding this notice contact her at (202) 622-3970 (not a toll-free call).

B-15: 1035 ASSIGNMENT LETTER

SAMPLE

ABSOLUTE ASSIGNMENT TO

XY INSURANCE COMPANY

AND

REQUEST FOR SURRENDER AS PART OF INTERNAL
REVENUE CODE SECTION 1035 EXCHANGE

OWNER/ASSIGNOR:
LIFE INSURANCE CONTRACT NUMBER :
CONTRACT ISSUED BY:

Assignment of Ownership

I, the undersigned, hereby state that I am the owner of the contract identified above. For the purpose of making an Internal Revenue Code section 1035 exchange of life insurance or annuity contract, I hereby absolutely assign and transfer all rigths, benefits, interests and property I have in the above identified contract to

XY INSURANCE COMPANY, ADDRESS hereafter «XY».

This assignment and section 1035 exchange is conditioned upon the decision by XY to issue, on the basis set forth in the application, a life insurance or annuity contract. After acceptance of the application by the underwriting department, this assignment will become absolute, and XY will issue me a life insurance Policy in exchange of the assignment of the above identified contract to XY. I understand that XY will, by the second section of this document, request the full and complete surrender of the above listed contract, and that the cash surrender value received from the surrender of the contract identified above will be credited to the XY contract upon receipt from the other company.

I understand that the contract values and terms of the above identified contract may differ substantially from those in the contract issued by XY.

I understand that XY will request the immediate surrender of the contract being assigned to them as part of the section 1035 exchange. If I elect to refuse the XY Policy under the «free look» provision, I recognize that the assigned contract may have already been surrendered for its cash value. If I refuse the policy under the «free look» provision, XY has no liability beyond the return of the cash surrender value of the assigned contract.

Neither XY nor any officer, employee, agent nor any person acting on behalf of XY warrants or represents the income tax consequences of this transaction. I have been advised by XY and /or its officers, agents, employees or persons acting on behalf of Valor Life that I should consult my own tax adviser regarding the tax consequences of this transaction. I have not relied on XY or any agent of VXY for tax advice.

Signed and effective this_____day of _____, 2010

Signature of Policy owner_____

NOTES

CHAPTER 2

1. Everbank, Foreign Currency Resources, 2010. www.everbank.com/002 Currency.aspx.
2. Ibid.
3. Ibid.
4. Ibid.
5. Ibid.
6. Ibid.
7. Ibid.
8. Ibid.
9. Ibid.
10. Ibid.
11. Ibid.
12. Ibid.
13. Ibid.
14. Ibid.
15. Ibid.
16. Ibid.
17. Ibid.
18. Ibid.

19. Ibid.
20. Ibid.
21. Ibid.
22. Ibid.
23. Ibid.
24. "New US Passport Rules Create Backlog as Applications Spike." March 19, 2007. www.workpermit.com/news/2007_03_19/us/passport_application_backlog.htm.
25. Weathcare—Asset Protection, "Threats to Your Wealth." www.wealthcare.com/asset_threats.html.
26. Darrell Aviss, "Obey 7 Rules to Protect Your Assets." www.chiroeco.com/news/chiropractic-news.php?id=3760.
27. American Bankruptcy Institute, www.abiworld.org/AM/Template.cfm?Section=Business_Bankruptcy_Filings1&Template=/TaggedPage/TaggedPageDisplay.cfm&TPLID=59&ContentID=36301.
28. PR Leap, "The Divorce Industry Costs Americans $28 Billion Dollars a Year." September 29, 2007. www.prleap.com/pr/96027/.
29. Economic Crimes Bureau, "Guarding Against Identity Theft." www.google.com/url?sa=t&source=web&ct=res&cd=3&ved=0CA8QFjAC&url=http%3A%2F%2Fwww.bnl.gov%2FHR%2FOCCMED%2FHPP%2Flinkable_files%2Fppt%2FGuarding_Against_Identity__Theft.ppt&ei=MyxdS6ObEY2OtgfMspyhAg&usg=AFQjCNHj2bFYy_HMaS2scVcVsdCfFFmefQ&sig2=p6HerVnQC_dAKjtugC4uiA.

CHAPTER 3

1. TIAA-CREF, Company History Page. www.tiaa-cref.org/about/press/about_us/history.html.
2. According to Article 65 of the Liechtenstein Rights Protection Act, gifts or gratuitous settlements made by a debtor are voidable preferences within one year after the initial transaction was made.
3. Article 67 of the Rights Protection Act mentions that there is no limitation in time, if the creditor can prove that the policyholder had the clear intent to defraud him as a creditor (possible only if he was insolvent at the time when he made the beneficiary designation), plus that the beneficiary knew about this intent. But, Article 74 Abs. 1 of the Rights Protection Act clearly states that five years after the transaction, the creditor loses his right for action of voidance.

CHAPTER 4

1. Zogby International: Ahead of the Curve, "A Growing Trend of Leaving America," July 28, 2008. www.zogby.com/templates/printsb.cfm?id= 17996.

CHAPTER 5

1. www.gov.im/.
2. Isle of Man Champion, www.isleofman.com/index.aspx.

GLOSSARY

Acceptance   Unconditional agreement by one party (the offeree) to the terms of an offer made by a second party (the offeror). Agreement results in a valid, binding contract.

Accumulation value   Similar to the concept of current market value for a mutual or exchange-traded fund, the accumulation value of a variable annuity is equivalent to the value of the policy's underlying portfolio, minus fees.

Annuitant   This term may refer to the person upon whom an annuity contract is based, or in other cases the individual named as beneficiary of an annuity or recipient of a pension.

Annuity   A financial contract offered by institutions (primarily insurers) that is designed to accept premiums, grow them through investment, and then pay a stream of payments to a named beneficiary at a designated point in time. American annuities are primarily used to supplement retirement income, whereas the foreign variety offer a much more robust range of benefits. Annuities are often relatively custom contracts, using a number of different templates based on prevailing tax law. The purpose of an offshore variable annuity is to allow investment flexibility and liquidity in addition to the promise of above-average returns thanks to worldwide access and prudent leadership.

Asset protection trust (APT)   A legal device allowing title to and possession of property to be held and/or managed by one person, the trustee, for the benefit of others, the beneficiaries, in order to protect the property from claims, judgments, and creditors.

Asset class   A group of securities or other investments that have similar characteristics. The most common classes are stocks, bonds, and cash equivalents; however, real estate, currencies, and commodities are also examples of an asset class.

Attachment   The postjudicial civil procedure by which personal property is taken from its owner pursuant to a judgment or other court order.

Bankruptcy   A court proceeding in which a debtor's assets are liquidated and the debtor is free of any further financial liability.

Basis   The original cost of an asset, later used to measure increased value for tax purposes at the time of sale or disposition.

Beneficiary   One designated to receive income from a trust or estate; a person named in an insurance policy to receive proceeds or benefits. With a policy, the beneficiary is named by the policyholder and may receive all or only some of the assets.

Bequest   A gift of personal property by will; also called a legacy.

Capital gain   The amount of profit earned from the sale or exchange of property, measured against the original cost basis.

Civil suit   A noncriminal legal action between parties relating to a dispute or injury seeking remedies for a violation of contractual or other personal rights.

Common law   The body of law developed in England from judicial decisions based on customs and precedent, constituting the basis of the present English, British Commonwealth, and U.S. legal systems.

Contingent beneficiary   The person or persons designated to receive the death benefit if the primary beneficiary dies prior to the death of the insured.

Contract   A binding agreement between two or more parties; also, the written or oral evidence of an agreement.

Creator   See *Grantor*.

Creditor   One to whom a debtor owes money or other valuable consideration.

Currency   Official, government-issued paper and coined money; hard currency describes a national currency sufficiently sound so as to be generally acceptable in international dealings.

Currency risk   The risk of an investment or business's market price or profit margins will be affected by fluctuations in prevailing currency exchange rates. For example, if an investment doubles in price, but the price of the underlying foreign currency falls by half, then the investor reaps no gain. Currency risk is a primary concern when investing in emerging markets, where currencies are less liquid and volatility greater.

Death benefit   The amount of money from a policy—life insurance or annuity—or pension that is paid out to the beneficiary when the insured person dies.

Debtor   One who owes another (the creditor) money or other valuable consideration or one who has neglected payments due.

Declaration   A formal statement in writing of any kind, often signed and notarized, especially a document establishing a trust; also called an indenture or trust agreement.

Deferred annuity   A type of annuity contract that delays payments of income, installments, or a lump sum until the investor elects to receive them. It becomes a deferred variable annuity when the policy is based not on a predetermined rate of return but on the value of an underlying portfolio.

Deferred life annuity   Payments are made at the end of a deferral period and continue for the lifetime of the insured person.

Domicile   A person's permanent legal home, as compared to a place that may be only a temporary residence. Domicile determines what law applies to the person for purposes of marriage, divorce, succession of estate at death, and taxation.

Estate   Any of various kinds or types of ownership a person may have in real or personal property; often used to describe all property of a deceased person, meaning the assets and liabilities remaining after death.

Estate tax   Taxes imposed at death by the United States and most state governments on assets of a decedent. The exempt amount by law reached $3.5 million in 2009, but it will be repealed in 2010 unless Congress votes to uphold the existing exemptions.

Exchange controls Government restrictions imposed on dealings in a national or foreign currency.

Executor A person who manages the estate of a decedent; also called a personal representative or administrator.

Exemption In tax law, a statutorily defined right to avoid imposition of part or all of certain taxes; also, the statutory right granted to a debtor in bankruptcy to retain a portion of his or her real or personal property free from creditors claims.

Expatriation The transfer of one's legal residence and citizenship from one's home country to another country, often in anticipation of government financial restrictions or taxes.

Family partnership (also known as **family limited partnership**) A legal business relationship created by agreement among two or more family members for a common purpose, often used as a means to transfer and/or equalize income and assets among family members so as to limit individual personal liability and taxes. See *Partnership* and *Limited partnership*.

Fiduciary A person holding title to property in trust for the benefit of another, as does a trustee, guardian, or executor of an estate.

Fixed annuity A simple contract that guarantees—in writing—a fixed rate of return during a buildup period followed by income payments for a fixed period of time or for life. This type of annuity, especially the Swiss fixed annuity, was popular in the 1980s thanks to high interest rates and a favorable tax situation; both of which have since changed.

Flight capital Movement of large sums of money across national borders, often in response to investment opportunities or to escape high taxes or pending political or social unrest; also called hot money.

Future interest An interest in property, usually real estate, possession and enjoyment of which is delayed until some future time or event; also, futures, securities, or goods bought or sold for future delivery, often keyed to price changes before delivery.

Gift tax U.S. tax imposed on any gift made by one person to another person annually in excess of US$10,000.

Grantor A person who conveys real property by deed; a person who creates a trust; also called a trust donor or settlor.

Grantor trust   As used in U.S. tax law, an offshore trust, the income of which is taxed by the IRS as the personal income of the grantor.

Gross estate   The total value for estate tax purposes of all a decedent's assets, as compared to net estate, the amount remaining after all permitted exemptions, deductions, taxes, and debts owed.

Haven or haven nation   A country where banking, tax, trust, and corporation laws are specially designed to attract foreign persons wishing to avoid taxes or protect assets.

Indices of ownership   Factors indicating a person's control over, and therefore ownership, especially of trust property, including the power of revocability.

Inheritance tax   A tax imposed by government on the amount a person receives from a decedent's estate, rather than on the estate itself. See *Estate tax.*

Inflation   A general rise in prices compared to the standard of level of purchasing power; often refers to an expansion to the monetary policy.

Insurance   A contract or policy under which a corporation (an insurer) undertakes to pay a specified amount of money in the event of a future damage or loss. Life insurance is a contract under which the insurer undertakes to indemnify or pay a person (the beneficiary) in the event of death of the insured for the insured payment of an established sum of money (the premium).

Insured person   In the context of life insurance, the individual on whose life the policy is based.

Interest   A right, title, or legal property share; also, a charge for borrowed money, usually a percentage of the total amount borrowed.

Interbank rate of exchange   The interest rate that banks charge each other in their dealings.

International financial center (used interchangeably with **offshore financial center**)   A term used to refer to a jurisdiction or city where major transnational financial service providers converge, often offering unparalleled access, opportunity, and a wide selection of products and rates. In virtually every case, these financial centers thrive in an environment of light regulation, low taxation, and a generally conservative—if not somewhat libertarian—atmosphere. Switzerland, Hong Kong, New York,

Singapore, and London are international financial centers known throughout the world.

Irrevocable trust A trust that, once established by the grantor, cannot be ended or terminated by the grantor.

IRS Form 720 The tax form used to report the purchase of any foreign annuity or life insurance policy to the International Revenue Service. A 1 percent excise tax is due on the purchase price of the annuity or life insurance policy.

Joint life annuity An annuity issued on two individuals under which payments continue in whole or in part until both individuals die.

Judgment An official and authenticated decision of a court.

Jurisdiction The statutory authority a court exercises; also, the geographic area or subject matter over which a government or court has power.

Last will and testament A written document in which a person directs the postmortem distribution of his or her property. In the United States, state law governs the specific requirements for a valid will.

Legal capacity The competency or ability of parties to make a valid contract, including being of majority age (18 years old) and of sound mind.

Life insurance A contract signed with an insurer, obligating it to pay a benefit of a certain value in case of death. Life insurance is also a favored vehicle among the wealthy for saving and investing, often under an umbrella of tax deferral.

Life insurance trust An irrevocable living trust that holds title to a policy on the grantor's life, proceeds from which are not part of the grantors estate.

Life estate The use and enjoyment of property granted by the owner to another during the owner's life, or during the life of another, at the termination of which title passes to another known as the remainderman.

Limited partnership A partnership in which individuals known as limited partners have no management role, but receive periodic income and are personally liable for partnership debts only to the extent of their individual investment.

Mutual fund A collective investment that pools money from multiple investors into multiple asset classes such as stocks, bonds, and other securities.

Mutual legal assistance treaty (MLAT)   Bilateral treaties between nations governing cooperation in international investigations of alleged criminal conduct.

Offshore   A general term used to refer to any foreign jurisdiction. More specifically, the term is often used in association with the world's offshore financial centers that offer services such as banking and insurance.

Power of attorney   A written instrument allowing one to act as agent on behalf of another, the scope of agency power indicated by the terms, known as general or limited powers.

Premium   The price paid by the policyholder to the insurer in exchange for the agreed benefits in the event of a claim or designated event.

Primary beneficiary   The individual designated as first to receive the proceeds of an insurance policy. There can be more than one primary beneficiary.

Probate   A series of judicial proceedings, usually in a special court, initially determining the validity of a last will and testament, then supervising the administration or execution of the terms of the will and the decedent's estate.

Private placement life insurance   A highly effective wealth-building and tax management strategy for high-net-worth individuals. It is best fit as a tool for tax management and investment flexibility, and it fits easily into a preexisting estate plan.

Property   Anything of value capable of being owned, including land (real property) and personal property, both tangible and intangible.

Protector   In offshore haven nations, an appointed person who has the duty of overseeing the activities of an offshore trust and its trustee.

Rate of return   The gain or loss of an investment over a specified period of time, expressed in terms of a percentage increase over the initial principal cost. Across all asset classes, rate of return serves as a key measure of an investment's performance.

Remainder   In testamentary law, the balance of an estate after payment of legacies; in property law, an interest in land or a trust estate distributed at the termination of a life estate. The person with a right to such an estate is the remainderman.

Revocable trust   A living trust in which the grantor retains the power to revoke or terminate the trust during his or her lifetime, returning the assets to him/herself.

Right of survivorship   An attribute of a joint tenancy that automatically transfers ownership of the share of a deceased joint tenant to surviving joint tenants without the necessity of probate.

Single life annuity   An annuity that provides income benefits for a single individual only.

Single-premium life insurance   Any form of life insurance funded by a single lump sum at the time of the policy's initiation.

Surrender   The early termination of an insurance product by the policyholder.

U.S. person   For U.S. tax purposes, any individual who is a U.S. citizen, a U.S. resident alien deemed to be a permanent resident, or a U.S. domiciled corporation, partnership, estate, or trust.

Variable annuity   An annuity solution designed to allow for a variable rate of return based on the performance of the underlying investments in the subaccount.

Withdrawal   The removal of some of the cash value in a private placement policy such as an annuity or life insurance contract.

1035 exchange   The tax-free transfer of funds from one insurance policy to another policy. This transaction has been approved by the IRS.

ABOUT THE AUTHORS

ERIKA NOLAN

Erika Nolan has been managing director for The Sovereign Society since its inception in 1998. She travels extensively throughout Europe, the Caribbean, and Central America in an effort to find the most knowledgeable financial experts and banking opportunities for Sovereign Society members. Erika's extensive knowledge of marketing and operational issues has helped grow membership to more than 25,000 individuals, expand the number of the Council of Experts to more than 44, and continuously improve the benefits and privileges Sovereign Society members cherish most. For more information about The Sovereign Society, visit www.sovereignsociety.com.

After spending nearly 10 years in the international asset protection and investment world, Erika saw a growing need to help people build and manage international wealth plans. In 2007, Erika cofounded N&C International Wealth Consultants, LLC, with Shannon Crouch. N&C specializes in researching and developing a comprehensive, worry-free strategy that will ensure that your wealth is properly protected and diversified. She is the coauthor of *Offshore Investments That Safeguard Your Cash* (McGraw Hill, 2008).

MARC-ANDRÉ SOLA

Marc-André Sola is a managing partner with NMG International Financial Services Ltd., a financial services company located in Zurich, Switzerland. Founded as a subsidiary of the NMG Group Inc., a financial services consulting group based in Singapore, with offices in 14 different countries, NMG International Financial Services Ltd. specializes in providing sophisticated investment structures for financial professionals and private investors and is the largest broker for private placement policies in Switzerland.

Marc-André holds a master of law degree at the University of Zurich and successfully combines his legal background with a vast experience in tailoring investment solutions for international investors. With more than 15 years of experience, Marc-André specializes in the areas of asset and privacy protection, estate planning, and tax-privileged investment solutions. Through his extensive network, Marc-André gives his clients access to the world's most reputable investment professionals, leading private banks, asset managers, and insurance companies. Marc-André is frequently invited to speak in front of international investors, investment professionals, and attorneys, and he is the author of a large number of articles on private placement policies and asset protection solutions.

SHANNON CROUCH

After graduating from Loyola College in Maryland, Shannon Crouch was recruited by Agora Publishing, one of the largest financial newsletter publishers in the United States, to oversee the marketing efforts for its largest division. In 1999, she was recruited by Erika Nolan and The Sovereign Society to oversee day-to-day operations and manage all publishing activities for the group.

In her 10-plus years with The Sovereign Society, Shannon has spent a considerable amount of time getting to know and understanding the needs of high-net-worth individuals and their families. She has traveled extensively throughout the world seeking out opportunities and contacts for members of The Sovereign Society. She is the coauthor of *Offshore Investments That Safeguard Your Cash* (McGraw Hill, 2008). In 2007, she cofounded N&C International Wealth Consultants, LLC, with Erika Nolan, and together they have just launched No Nonsense Marketing, LLC, working with financial advisers.

INDEX